101 Brie Recipes

(101 Brie Recipes - Volume 1)

Debora Molino

Copyright: Published in the United States by Debora Molino/ © DEBORA MOLINO

Published on December, 02 2020

All rights reserved. No part of this publication may be reproduced, stored in retrieval system, copied in any form or by any means, electronic, mechanical, photocopying, recording or otherwise transmitted without written permission from the publisher. Please do not participate in or encourage piracy of this material in any way. You must not circulate this book in any format. DEBORA MOLINO does not control or direct users' actions and is not responsible for the information or content shared, harm and/or actions of the book readers.

In accordance with the U.S. Copyright Act of 1976, the scanning, uploading and electronic sharing of any part of this book without the permission of the publisher constitute unlawful piracy and theft of the author's intellectual property. If you would like to use material from the book (other than just simply for reviewing the book), prior permission must be obtained by contacting the author at author@rosemaryrecipes.com

Thank you for your support of the author's rights.

Content

101 AWESOME BRIE RECIPES 5

1. ANT HILL 5
2. Asparagus And Brie Risotto With Brown Butter Almonds 5
3. BLT Casserole 6
4. Baked Brie With Caramelized Onions & Wild Mushrooms 6
5. Baked Brie With Chai Date Spread 7
6. Baked Brie In Homemade Pie Crust 7
7. Baked Brie In Puff Pastry With Cranberries, Pistachios & Sumac 8
8. Baked Brie With Fresh Blueberries 9
9. Baked Brie With Raspberries & Rosemary . 9
10. Berry And Brie American Flag Appetizer . 10
11. Blueberry Brie Risotto 10
12. Brie & Grape Tart 10
13. Brie & Apple Tart With Medjool Crunch And A Gruyere Crust 11
14. Brie En Croute 12
15. Brie En Croute Stuffed With Date Jam 12
16. Brie Fig Ice Cream 12
17. Brie Pear And Apricot Sammie With Sweet Thai Dipping Sauce 13
18. Brie And Butter Grits With Honey And Raspberry Compote 13
19. Brie And Date Paste Pizza 14
20. Brie And Prosciutto Melt 14
21. Brie And Onion Jam Crostini 14
22. Brie Stuffed With Dried Fruits And Nuts . 15
23. Brie With Cherry Chipotle Chutney 15
24. Brioche Circles With Brie And Cherries ... 16
25. Buckwheat Crepes With Brie + Honey Sauteed Swiss Chard 17
26. Caramelized Apple Tart With Brie Puff Pastry (Tarte Tatin) 18
27. Caramelized Pear And Melted Brie On Brioche 18
28. Cavatappi With Sun Dried Tomatoes, Brie & Arugula 19
29. Cheese Plate 19
30. Cranberry Brie Crescent Wreath 20
31. Cranberry Brie Puff Pastries 21
32. Cranberry Chipotle Marmalade 22
33. Cream Of Brie Soup 22
34. Creamy Avocado And Brie Sandwich 23
35. Croissants Filled With Brie & Strawberries 23
36. Dan Rooney's Signature Burger 23
37. Duck Confit, Pear, And Fennel Bites 23
38. Dutch Mustard Soup 24
39. Em's Buns 24
40. Fiesta Bruschetta 26
41. Fig, Brie & Prosciutto Pizza 26
42. Fig, Prosciutto And Brie Puffs 27
43. Flamiche Au Maroilles Avec Pêche 27
44. French Toast With Pears, Blood Orange Caramel Sauce, And Brie 27
45. French Baguette Sandwich 28
46. Fusilli With Fresh Heirloom Tomatoes And Brie 28
47. Grape And Brie Barley Salad 29
48. Grilled Brie Sandwiches With Honey, Pistachio & Kale Pesto 29
49. Grilled Brie Topped With Slow Roasted Sunblushed Tomatoes 30
50. Grilled Carrot And Chickpea Panzanella With Brie 31
51. Grilled Chicken Burger With Brie 32
52. Guilty Pleasure Lunch 32
53. Honeyed Pear And Brie Toasts 32
54. Individual Apple Brie Pies Tartlets 33
55. LA VICTORIA Pineapple Verde Baked Brie 33
56. La Pearisienne 33
57. Leek, Mushroom, And Roma Fritatta With Brie 34
58. Maple Brie Sweet Potato Gratin 34
59. Mini Phyllo Wrapped Brie With Honey And Pistachios 35
60. Montrachet Tarts 35
61. Mushroom Soup With Red Wine And Brie 36
62. Mushroom Soup With Wheat Berries, Kale, And Brie 36
63. Pasta With Tomatoes, Garlic, Basil & Brie 37
64. Pear Bacon And Brie Crust....eenies 38
65. Pear, Ham And Brie Galette 38
66. Persimmon Grilled Cheese W/ Goat Cheddar & Prosciutto 38

67. Polenta Cakes With Caramelized Onions, Brie And Basil Oil 39
68. Pumpkin Bread With Brie 39
69. Red Onion & Apple Gastrique Tartlets 40
70. Roast Turkey, Brie, Cranberry Sandwich On Walnut Bread 41
71. Roasted Garlic Baked Brie 41
72. Roasted Garlic And Brie Toasts 42
73. Roasted Garlic, Avocado, Brie And Green Sauce Dip 42
74. Roasted Garlic, Onion & Chicken Soup ... 43
75. Roasted Pineapple Heirloom Tomato And Brie Bruschetta 44
76. Roasted Beet And Brie Sandwich 44
77. Sauteed Brie And Shrimp 44
78. Savory Asian Pear, Onion And Fennel Galette 45
79. Savory Crescents With Brie, Apples And Date Berry Sauce 46
80. Smoked Apple & Brie Cheese Cake 46
81. Smoked Jalapeño Poppers With Bacon, Apple, And Brie 47
82. Steak Sandwich With Peach "jam" And Brie 48
83. Summer Tomato Linguine With Brie And Basil 48
84. Sweet & Savory "Vesper" Bread 49
85. Sweetbreads Crostini With On Hand Chimichurri 49
86. TB Cubed 50
87. TURKEY + BRIE + AVOCADO BURGER 50
88. Tawny Port Two Cheese Spread 51
89. The Pink Poodle Pizza 51
90. Tomato & Brie Pasta 52
91. Tomato And Basil Pasta With Brie 52
92. Tomato And Brie Tart 52
93. Tropical Mango Salsa With Proscuitto Wrapped Shrimp 53
94. Turkey, Brie & Peach Panini 53
95. Watercress, Pear, And Brie Salad 54
96. White Cheddar Fig Grilled Cheese 54
97. Wild Mushroom Onion Galette With Brie 55
98. Yellow Oyster Mushrooms On A Brie Toast 55
99. Brie, Pear And Arugula Sandwich 56

100. Pom.brie.crostini 56
101. Toasty TBBB 56

INDEX **58**

CONCLUSION **61**

101 Awesome Brie Recipes

***

1. ANT HILL

Serving: Serves 2 | Prep: | Cook: | Ready in:

Ingredients

- 8 ounces BRIE
- 1 cup RAISINS
- 4 ounces CARAMEL SAUCE

Direction

- Place whole round or triangle brie on dish.
- Pour 2oz of caramel sauce on top of brie
- Pour 1 cup of raisins on top brie
- Top brie and raisins with the other 2 oz of brie

2. Asparagus And Brie Risotto With Brown Butter Almonds

Serving: Serves 6 or 4 | Prep: | Cook: | Ready in:

Ingredients

- Risotto
- 4 cups homemead or low sodium chicken stock
- 1 large shallot minced
- 1+ tablespoons butter
- 1.5 cups Canaroli rice
- 3/4 cup dry white wine or vermouth
- 1/2 pound fresh asparagus
- 1/4 pound chilled Brie de Meaux or other creamy lovely brie
- 1 tablespoon lemon zest
- 1/4 cup grated parmesean
- Brown Butter Almonds
- 3/4 slivered almonds
- 2.5 tablespoons Butter
- 2 tablespoons lemon juice

Direction

- Risotto
- Set stock over medium heat, add lemon zest heat to a simmer
- Cut tips off asparagus, cut stems into thin circles, cut brie into 1" cubes (I leave the rind in)
- Set a wide sauté pan over medium and heat, 1 Tbsp. butter, add shallots, season with salt & white pepper sweat till soft and translucent
- Add rice and stir together, making sure all the grains are coated in butter and shiny, when they become like little pearls raise heat a bit and pour in the wine, stir and let it absorb into the rice once all the wine has been absorbed, ladle in some hot stock. Stir gently and consistently, when that has been absorbed and in some more, keep going, let the rice get thirsty then add in more stock
- As the swells and becomes creamy, test every so often when it is just a moment sort of al dente (the tiny white bit in the center is barely there) add the asparagus then one more ladle of stock, stir and cover for a minute or two
- Remove cover, lower heat stir in brie and grated parmesan. Let in melt and ooze into the rice, stir till the rind has disappeared, if you think it needs it stir in a cube or two of butter. Season with Salt & Cracked Black Pepper
- To serve; keep warm and pour almonds & brown butter over top, garnish with chopped chives and fresh cracked peppers
- Brown Butter Almonds
- Set heavy bottomed sauté pan over medium heat
- Add almonds, shake or stir until they just start to brown

- Add lemon juice, let it evaporate
- Remove almonds, add butter, lower heat and let butter brown, when it is fragrant & nutty add almond back.

3. BLT Casserole

Serving: Serves 6 | Prep: | Cook: | Ready in:

Ingredients

- 1 1/2 pounds applewood smoked bacon
- 1 1/2 pounds hardwood smoked slab bacon
- 1 pound triple cream brie
- 12 tablespoons dijon mustard
- 3-4 pints grape tomatoes (8-10 tomatoes per casserole)
- 6 small leeks
- 4 large shallots
- 1/4 cup dry white wine
- 1/4 cup olive oil
- salt and pepper to taste
- 6 individual casserole dishes

Direction

- Place the apple wood bacon on a wire rack, on top of a cookie sheet, and bake at 400 degrees for 20-30 minutes till cooked, but not crisp. Slice into ribbons. Don't discard the rendered bacon fat. At the same time, cut each tomato in half and place them on a baking sheet. Rub the tomatoes with olive oil, salt, and pepper, and place them in the oven with the bacon. After 10 minutes, turn the tomatoes and cook for another 10 minutes. They should be done about the same time as the bacon.
- Slice the leek and shallots into rounds and put in a colander. Run water over them to remove any dirt and pat dry. Sauté in the rendered bacon fat till translucent and remove from pan. Put the remaining bacon fat in a small bowl.
- . Chop the slab bacon into ¼ inch cubes and sauté till done, but not crispy.
- Lightly grease the casserole dishes with bacon fat. Place phyllo on a cutting board, the long way down. Cut into 6 even squares (2 across, 3 down). Place 5 ungreased sheets in the bottom of each casserole dish.
- Distribute the slab bacon evenly among each dish. Place 2 layers of ungreased phyllo over the bacon. Put 2 tbsp. Dijon mustard on the phyllo and spread evenly. Distribute the leeks evenly over the Dijon mustard. Distribute the tomatoes evenly over the leeks. Distribute the ribbons of bacon evenly over the tomatoes. Distribute the brie sauce evenly over the top of each casserole. Place 1 layer of phyllo over each casserole. With a pastry brush, brush the bacon fat on the phyllo. Repeat with 4 more layers of phyllo and bacon fat.
- Bake on a cookie sheet for 15-20 minutes, or until phyllo is browned and casserole is bubbly. Let rest 10 minutes before serving. Makes 6 large servings.

4. Baked Brie With Caramelized Onions & Wild Mushrooms

Serving: Serves 6 | Prep: 0hours20mins | Cook: 0hours15mins | Ready in:

Ingredients

- 2 tablespoons extra-virgin olive oil, plus 2 tablespoons
- 1 medium sized brown onion, thinly sliced
- 1/2 teaspoon brown sugar
- 5 sprigs thyme
- 1 bay leaf
- 1/2 cup red wine
- 3 cups assortment of wild mushrooms, cleaned
- Salt and pepper, to taste
- 1 medium sized wheel of good quality brie
- baguettes and crackers, to serve

Direction

- Begin by heating the oven to 350F.
- Next, caramelize the onion on the stovetop with the brown sugar and extra-virgin olive oil. About 6 minutes into cooking the onions, toss in the thyme, bay leaf and the red wine.
- At this point, pop your brie in the freezer, for about 7 minutes. This will harden it up a bit, making it easier to remove the top rind later.
- Chop your mushrooms into smaller pieces—depending on the size of your mushrooms it will vary, but you want to aim for pieces that are small enough to pick up with a cracker, but not too small.
- Add the mushrooms to the onion mixture, along with more extra-virgin olive oil. Cook the mixture down for about 7 minutes. Add salt and pepper to taste.
- While the mushroom mixture is cooking, cover a small baking tin with two layers of foil. Put the brie into the baking tin, and scrape the top rind off of the brie—because you've frozen it, this process is much easier and you won't lose as much brie. And the removed rind makes for excellent snacking while you assemble the rest of the dish!
- Spread the mushroom and onion mixture evenly across the brie, and pop it into the oven.
- After about 12 minutes, when the brie is bubbling slightly including in the center, remove the brie from the oven. Serve immediately with plenty of bread and crackers for dunking—absolutely delicious!

5. Baked Brie With Chai Date Spread

Serving: Serves 2-3 | Prep: | Cook: | Ready in:

Ingredients

- 200 grams Brie cheese
- 200 grams Date
- 1 cup hot water
- 8 pieces Cardamom (pod)
- 8 pieces Cloves (pod)
- 1 piece Cinnamon (Stick)
- 8 pieces Peppercorn
- 1 piece Fresh ginger
- 1 tablespoon Tea leaves

Direction

- Soak 200g dates with 1 cup of hot water and set aside.
- Pre-heat the oven to 180c for 10 minutes.
- Remove any plastic wrap on Brie (don't remove the white rind on cheese itself) and bake for 8-10 minutes.
- Let it cool down for 15-20 minutes.
- Prepare Chai by adding all spices, and tea leaves together with a cup of water on medium heat in a small pot for 5-10 minutes.
- Strain Chai to have clear liquid, and mix it with date spread in the blender.
- Now just spread it over brie, add toasted almonds and enjoy!
- You can jam and crackers also with brie

6. Baked Brie In Homemade Pie Crust

Serving: Serves varies | Prep: | Cook: | Ready in:

Ingredients

- 1/2 cup all-purpose or white whole wheat flour
- 1/2 teaspoon sugar
- 1/8 teaspoon table salt
- 2.5 tablespoons butter, very cold
- 2-3 tablespoons ice water
- 8-14 ounces wheel of brie
- 3-4 tablespoons jam
- 1 teaspoon milk or egg, optional
- 2 tablespoons sliced almonds, optional

Direction

- In a small bowl, whisk together the flour, sugar and salt. Cut the butter into 1/4-inch cubes and sprinkle over the dough. Using your fingers, pinch the cubes between your fingers while stirring, working to distribute the smashed butter throughout the flour. Your goal is to have as many tiny flakes of butter distributed throughout the flour as possible — try not to leave any big chunks of butter, or your pie crust may end up with greasy holes.
- Add 2 tablespoons of ice water and stir until a soft dough comes together. The dough should be slightly sticky and very soft, but not unmanageable. Add more water, a teaspoon at a time, if your dough seems too dry.
- Cover with plastic wrap and let rest in the fridge for at least 20 minutes.
- A few minutes before the dough is done resting, preheat your oven to 400F. On a lightly floured surface or between two pieces of plastic wrap, roll out the dough until it is large enough to cover your wheel of brie. If you have a smaller wheel, you may be able to entirely enclose the brie with your dough. With my 13.5 oz. wheel, I was only able to cover the top and sides of the brie, tucking the edges underneath.
- Shave some of the rind off the top of the wheel if you like (leave the bottom intact for your best chance at minimizing cheese ooze) and spread liberally with jam. Enclose the wheel in dough, leaving the jam side up. Brush the pie dough with a few teaspoons of milk or a bit of egg. Top with sliced almonds if desired — they'll toast in the oven.
- Bake for 15-20 minutes, or until crust is golden brown. Remove from oven and drizzle with honey. Let sit for 5 minutes before serving.

7. Baked Brie In Puff Pastry With Cranberries, Pistachios & Sumac

Serving: Makes 1 baked brie | Prep: 0hours30mins | Cook: 0hours50mins | Ready in:

Ingredients

- 1 cup frozen cranberries
- 1/4 cup orange juice
- 2 tablespoons honey (or to taste)
- 1 1/2 teaspoons sumac, divided
- 1 pinch kosher salt
- 1 sheet frozen puff pastry, thawed according to package directions
- 1 round brie (about 8 ounces), chilled (white rind trimmed, if you like)
- 1/4 cup shelled pistachios, toasted and roughly chopped
- 1 egg, beaten with 1 tablespoon water

Direction

- To make the cranberry jam: Combine cranberries, orange juice, honey, 1 teaspoon sumac, and a pinch of salt in a saucepan; bring to a boil over medium-high heat. Lower heat, and let simmer until the berries burst, most of the liquid evaporates, and the sauce thickens, about 8 to 10 minutes, stirring several times so it doesn't burn. Remove from heat and let cool.
- Heat oven to 400°F.
- Roll out the thawed sheet of puff pastry to about 1/8-inch thickness. Place brie in center of pastry. Spread about 2 tablespoons of the cranberry jam over the top of the cheese, then sprinkle about half of the pistachios on top of the jam. Fold one edge of the dough over the brie, then the opposite side. Fold the remaining edges across the brie to completely encase it. (Note: the dough should just cover the brie; trim off excess pieces of dough, if necessary, to ensure the pastry evenly browns and crisps.) Place wrapped brie on a parchment-lined baking sheet.

- Brush the egg wash over the top and sides of the brie. Sprinkle with the remaining 1/2 teaspoon of sumac. Bake on the center rack for about 25 to 35 minutes, or until the pastry is golden brown and cooked through. (The cheese may leak through – this is fine!)
- Transfer to a wire rack and let cool for about 5 to 10 minutes. Serve warm with extra cranberry jam and pistachios on the side.

8. Baked Brie With Fresh Blueberries

Serving: Serves 4 dessert slices | Prep: | Cook: | Ready in:

Ingredients

- 1 baby brie (about 8oz)
- 1/2 cup fresh blueberries
- 2 tablespoons honey
- 4 tablespoons unsalted butter, softened
- 1 8oz roll of phyllo dough, thawed

Direction

- In a small saucepan, place half of the berries, along with the honey and 1 tbsp water on medium heat. Stir frequently for about 5 minutes, or until the berries have broken down. Set this aside to cool.
- Use a knife to scrape off the wax on the wheel of cheese. You don't have to get it all off, but I like to do this to ensure that the cheese combines better with the berry mixture.
- Lay out a few layers of the phyllo dough. Place the cheese on top. Pour enough of the berry mixture on top to cover the brie. You might not use all of it here, but you can serve any leftover alongside the finished brie. Then place the remaining fresh berries on top of this.
- From here, you're going to lovingly layer a few pieces of phyllo at a time, like wrapping a small gift. Use the butter as your tape to hold the layers in place. Flip the cheese back and forth as you do this (so that all the tucked in pieces are not all on the same side), but be careful to remember which side is up.
- Place the berry side up on a greased baking sheet. Brush a layer of butter on the outer layer. You can save this brie baby in the fridge like this to bake at a later time. When you're ready, bake it for about 20 minutes at 350F or until crisp and brown on the outside.

9. Baked Brie With Raspberries & Rosemary

Serving: Serves 8 | Prep: | Cook: | Ready in:

Ingredients

- 1/2 cup raspberry preserves
- 1/4 cup raspberries, fresh
- 1 teaspoon fresh rosemary leaves, minced
- Ground black pepper
- 1 sheet frozen puff pastry (half of a 17.3-oz. package), thawed
- 1 13-ounce brie round (approx. 6-7" in diameter)
- 1 large egg, beaten
- Crackers, baguette slices, grapes

Direction

- Preheat oven to 400 degrees F.
- In a small bowl, blend the preserves, raspberries and rosemary. Season with ground pepper (to taste).
- On a lightly floured surface, roll out the pastry dough to make a 12" square.
- Cut off the top rind of the cheese wheel. Discard the rind.
- Place the brie (rindless side up) in the center of the pastry, and spoon the raspberry mixture on top of the cheese.
- Starting with two opposite corners, fold twos sides of the pastry over the cheese.
- Brush the remaining two sides with egg glaze, and fold over the cheese. Press seams to seal, and brush the pastry with egg glaze.

- Place the pastry-wrapped cheese on a baking sheet, and bake in the preheated oven until the pastry turns golden brown: approx. 30 minutes. Note: The top of the pastry may split open during the baking process.
- Once removed from the oven, allow the dish to cool on the backing sheet for 20 minutes. Place baked cheese on a serving platter, and serve with crackers, toasted baguette slices and grapes.

10. Berry And Brie American Flag Appetizer

Serving: Serves 6-8 | Prep: | Cook: | Ready in:

Ingredients

- 1 package puff pastry, defrosted per the package instructions
- 1/2 pound strawberries, thinly sliced
- 1/2 cup blueberries, halved
- 1 wedge Brie, thinly sliced
- 2 tablespoons melted butter

Direction

- Preheat the oven to 375 degrees Fahrenheit.
- Flour your prep surface and carefully roll out the pastry into a large rectangle. Use a pizza cutter to cut the pastry into rectangles and transfer to a cooking sprayed baking sheet.
- Carefully layer two pieces of Brie on each rectangle, followed by strawberry slivers and blueberries made out to look like the flag. Brush the edges of the pastry with melted butter.
- Bake for 15 minutes or so, watching carefully, until lightly browned. Remove from the oven and cool slightly before serving.

11. Blueberry Brie Risotto

Serving: Serves 6 | Prep: | Cook: | Ready in:

Ingredients

- 4-5 cups Vegetable Stock
- 1/2 cup Red Wine
- 1 carton Blueberries, washed and pureed
- 1/3 cup Brie Cheese, without the rind
- 1/2 teaspoon Kosher Salt

Direction

- Heat the vegetable or chicken stock and set aside.
- In a sauté pan, add red wine and rice. Cook on medium and gently stir the rice until the wine has almost been absorbed. Add one ladle-ful of stock and continue to stir. When the liquid has almost been absorbed, add another ladle-ful of stock. Continue this process until approximately 4-5 cups of stock have been used. The rice should be "al dente" and creamy, not mushy. If the rice is too firm, add more stock until you reach the desired firmness.
- At this point, add the pureed blueberries, salt and brie and stir until the cheese has completely melted. Serve immediately.

12. Brie & Grape Tart

Serving: Makes one 11" tart | Prep: | Cook: | Ready in:

Ingredients

- Crust
- 1 cup all-purpose flour, plus more for dusting surface
- 2/3 cup plus 1 teaspoon yellow cornmeal
- 2 teaspoons baking powder
- 1/4 teaspoon table salt
- 2 tablespoons extra virgin olive oil

- 1/2 cup water
- Tart topping
- 1/2 tablespoon extra virgin olive oil
- 1 ounce finely grated pecorino romano cheese
- 1 teaspoon finely chopped fresh rosemary, divided
- 4 ounces of your favorite brie cheese
- 10-15 seedless red grapes, cut into quarters (pole to pole)
- 1 to 2 tablepsoons pine nuts

Direction

- Crust
- Heat oven to 400 F, with rack in the lowest position. Whisk flour, 2/3 cup cornmeal, baking powder and salt together in a medium bowl. Make a well in the center of the dry ingredients, and add the oil and water. Using wooden spoon mix together to form a dough.
- Turn dough out onto lightly floured surface. Knead for several minutes, dusting with more flour to create a homogenous dough that is slightly tacky.
- Roll dough into 10-11" circle on a piece of parchment paper.
- Sprinkle 1 teaspoon cornmeal over the bottom of the tart pan. Transfer dough into pan, using the parchment paper to turn dough into pan. Peel off parchment, then pat dough into the edges of the pan.
- Tart topping
- Drizzle the olive oil onto the crust, then use a pastry brush to spread it. Sprinkle on the romano cheese in an even layer. Sprinkle about 2/3 of the rosemary over the cheese.
- Cut the brie into approximately 1/8-inch thick slices. Cut each slice into 3-4 pieces, so each piece is roughly square. Arrange the pieces evenly over the surface of the crust, staying 1/2-inch away from the edges.
- Scatter the grape slivers and pine nuts over the surface of the tart. Bake on lowest rack of oven for 13-15 minutes, until the very edges of the tart just start to brown and pull away from the pan. Sprinkle with remaining rosemary, slice, and serve.

13. Brie & Apple Tart With Medjool Crunch And A Gruyere Crust

Serving: Serves 8-10 | Prep: | Cook: | Ready in:

Ingredients

- Gruyere crust
- 3/4 cup all purpose flour
- 6 tablespoons butter, in chunks
- 1/4 cup gruyere cheese, grated
- 5 teaspoons cold water
- Brie, apple, and medjool crunch
- 1 green apple, as thinly sliced as possible
- 1 block of brie (200g) cut into thin slices
- 1/3 cup ground hazelnuts
- 1/3 cup ground almonds
- 6 medjool dates, pitted
- 1 tablespoon butter
- 1 teaspoon honey

Direction

- Mix flour and chopped butter in a large bowl, until the texture of the mixture looks like breadcrumbs. Stir in the grated gruyere.
- Slowly sprinkle water over the flour mixture, one teaspoon at a time, making sure there is enough water to form the dough. Form the dough into a ball, wrap it in plastic wrap and refrigerate it for at least 45 min.
- Preheat the oven to 375 F (190 C) and roll the dough out into a 9-inch pie pan. Use a fork to prick holes in the crust.
- Bake in preheated oven for 12 minutes.
- Brie, apple, and medjool crunch
- First, make the medjool crunch in your food processor. Pulse together dates, hazelnuts, almonds, and butter until the mixture comes together. It will look kind of like quinoa.
- Arrange the apples in a single layer on the gruyere crust. Drizzle the apples with the honey.

- Layer the thinly-sliced brie on the apples, then sprinkle the medjool crunch over the brie.
- Bake in the preheated oven at 375 F for 15 minutes, or until the brie has melted. Drizzle some honey on top and serve hot.

14. Brie En Croute

Serving: Serves 6 to 8 | Prep: 0hours10mins | Cook: 0hours15mins | Ready in:

Ingredients

- 1 Medium Brie, entire wheel
- 1 Sheet Puff Pastry, I love Dufour
- 1 cup chopped pecans
- 1 cup dried craisins
- 1/2 cup brown sugar
- 1 egg, beaten with 1 tablespoon water

Direction

- Cut Brie in half lengthwise. Sprinkle all other ingredients inside starting with brown sugar. Place top of brie on top and press down.
- Roll out puff pastry sheet and place brie in middle. Wrap the brie up with the puff pastry and turn over.
- Place brie in freezer for at least an hour so puff pastry refreezes.
- Heat oven to 425. Place parchment paper on a sheet tray with brie on top and brush top and side with egg wash.
- Heat in oven for at least 15 minutes. Brie is done when the puff pastry is evenly brown on all sides and puffed.
- To serve, place on a large platter with crackers, small cheese knives and cut bread. Cut a small wedge out so the melty goodness starts to pour out. Eat the sliver you cut before guests arrive, it will be the only piece you get!

15. Brie En Croute Stuffed With Date Jam

Serving: Serves 6-8 | Prep: | Cook: |Ready in:

Ingredients

- 16 ounces wheel of Brie
- 1 piece frozen puff pastry
- 2 tablespoons date jam
- 1 egg, beaten with 1 tablespoon of water
- flour, as needed for rolling

Direction

- Preheat oven to 400° F
- With a sharp knife, cut brie wheel in half so that you can open it like a book (This is easiest when the brie is cold).
- Spread the inside of the bottom half of the brie with the date jam, then place the other half on top, like you're making a brie sandwich. Set aside.
- Sprinkle a little flour on a flat work surface and unfold the sheet of puff pastry. Sprinkle the top of the sheet and your rolling pin with some flour and proceed to roll it out until it measures about 12"x12".
- Place brie, topside down, onto the center of the puff pastry. Gently gather the corners of the pastry sheet in towards the middle, enclosing the brie in the pastry. Slowly transfer brie to a sheet pan that's been sprayed with non-stick spray, seam side down. Gently gather in any protruding edges towards the brie, so that it's in the shape of a rough circle. Brush the pastry all over with the egg wash. Transfer pan to the oven and bake for 35 min, until pastry is golden brown and brie is melted and oozing inside. Let rest 10 min before carving.

16. Brie Fig Ice Cream

Serving: Makes "generous 1 quart" | Prep: | Cook: | Ready in:

Ingredients

- Brie Ice Cream Mix
- 2 cups whole milk
- 1 tablespoon 1 tsn cornstarch
- 6 ounces brie cheese, rind removed
- 2 tablespoons Naefchatel cheese
- 1.25 cups heavy cream
- 2/3 cup sugar
- 1/4 cup light corn syrup
- 1 fig sauce
- Fig Sauce
- 3/4 cup fresh fig seeds (druplets)
- 2 tablespoons sugar

Direction

- Mix about 2 tbsp milk with cornstarch in small bowl to make a smooth slurry," divide brie and Naefchatel cheese into tiny pieces and mix together in a large bowl
- Combine remaining milk, the cream, sugar, and corn syrup in a 4 quart saucepan, bring to a rolling boil over m-h heat and boil for 4 min. Remove from heat & gradually whisk in cornstarch slurry, bring mixture back to boiling over m-h heat, stirring with a rubber spatula until thickened, about 1 min. remove from heat"
- Gradually whisk hot milk mixture into cheese mixture until smooth." whisk well with each small addition of the hot milk mixture to ensure smoothness. Cover and chill in refrigerator while ice cream make in freezer overnight.
- Pour ice cream based into frozen ice cream maker until thick and creamy. Pack... into storage container, alternating with" fig sauce. "Do not mix. Press a sheet of" wax paper "directly against the surface, and seal with an airtight lid." Freeze overnight
- Fig Sauce
- Heat in small saucepan over medium high heat until well combined, remove from heat and allow it to cool before use. If making for brie ice cream, it's best to make before ice cream is put into ice cream maker. It can cool as you are spinning the ice cream.

17. Brie Pear And Apricot Sammie With Sweet Thai Dipping Sauce

Serving: Serves 1 | Prep: | Cook: | Ready in:

Ingredients

- 1 tablespoon softened butter
- 2 slices sourdough bread
- 4 ounces brie, sliced into 4 slices, about 1 1/2 to 2 ounces
- 2 tablespoons apricot preserves
- 1 ripe pear, thinly sliced.
- 1 tablespoon sweet thai chili sauce
- 1 tablespoon marmelade
- 1 teaspoon hot sauce

Direction

- Spread softened butter on one side of each of the slices of sourdough.
- Spread preserves on the unbuttered side.
- Arrange brie over preserves, then some thin slices of pear.

18. Brie And Butter Grits With Honey And Raspberry Compote

Serving: Serves 2 | Prep: | Cook: | Ready in:

Ingredients

- Brie and Butter Grits
- 1 cup water
- 1/2 cup milk (I use low-fat)
- 1 pinch salt
- 1/2 cup grits or polenta
- 1 tablespoon butter
- 2 tablespoons Brie cheese

- 2 to 3 tablespoons honey
- Raspberry Compote
- 1/3 cup fresh or frozen raspberries
- 2 tablespoons brown sugar
- 2 tablespoons slivered almonds

Direction

- In a medium pot, bring the water, milk and salt to a boil. Add the grits and lower to a simmer, stirring occasionally. After 2 minutes, add the butter, the Brie, and 2 tablespoons of the honey. Taste to adjust the sweetness according to your preference. Simmer for another 3 to 4 minutes and serve in a bowl.
- For the raspberry compote, simply add the raspberries and the sugar to a small pot and simmer until thickened, about 3 minutes. Top the grits with the slivered almonds, raspberries, and add a bit more honey or brown sugar if desired. Enjoy!

19. Brie And Date Paste Pizza

Serving: Serves 4 | Prep: | Cook: | Ready in:

Ingredients

- 1/3 cup date paste
- .4 pounds brie (I used St. Angel)
- 1 handful Arugula
- 2 slices prosciutto
- 1 pizza dough
- 1/4 cup toasted walnuts

Direction

- 1. Preheat the oven to 425.
- 2. Roll out your pizza dough and place on a baking sheet then prick with a fork.
- 3. Bake the crust for 5 minutes or until you can gently lift the side of the crust and it comes up easily.
- 4. Spread the date paste across the crust like you would tomato sauce
- 5. Top with slices of the brie and place back in the oven until the cheese has begun to pool (this took around 6 minutes for me)
- 6. Scatter walnuts, arugula, and prosciutto on top of the warm pizza and slice.

20. Brie And Prosciutto Melt

Serving: Serves 1 | Prep: | Cook: | Ready in:

Ingredients

- 2 pieces thickly sliced brioche
- 1 teaspoon butter
- 2 ounces brie
- 2 pieces thinly sliced proscuitto
- 1 teaspoon butter

Direction

- Melt the butter on the flat side of a griddle pan or frying pan over a medium heat and place the 2 slices of brioche in the pan. Remove once lightly browned.
- Top one of the browned sides with 50g/2oz sliced brie a couple of slices of prosciutto (or other ham) and top with the other slice of brioche, browned side down. Melt the other teaspoon of butter in the pan and place the sandwich back in. Rest another heavy pan on top to press down. After about 30 seconds (or once lightly browned) flip over and again press using a heavy pan. Remove from the pan and serve immediately.

21. Brie And Onion Jam Crostini

Serving: Serves 12 crostini | Prep: | Cook: | Ready in:

Ingredients

- 1 Large red onion, thinly sliced
- 2 teaspoons Olive oil

- 1/2 teaspoon Salt
- 1/4 teaspoon Mustard powder
- 2 teaspoons Brown sugar
- 3 tablespoons Balsamic vinegar
- 2 sprigs Fresh thyme chopped
- few grinds of black pepper
- 1 Baguette
- 1 Wheel or log of Brie
- 2 tablespoons Chopped walnuts

Direction

- In a large frying pan, warm the oil and then add onion slices. Sprinkle with a nice pinch of salt and gently cook over medium low heat until deeply brown. This will take about 20 minutes. Be patient this needs to be done low and slow.
- Add the mustard powder, brown sugar, pepper, thyme and vinegar. Cook, stirring often until vinegar evaporates, about 5 minutes. Set aside until ready to assemble crostini.
- Cut the baguette into 3/4 inch slices brush with olive oil. Toast at 350 degrees until golden. Slice the Brie into twelve pieces.
- On each crostini spread onion jam, place a piece of Brie and sprinkle walnuts on top. Bake in the oven a few minutes until cheese is slightly melted but not runny. Serve immediately.

22. Brie Stuffed With Dried Fruits And Nuts

Serving: Makes 1 cheese | Prep: | Cook: | Ready in:

Ingredients

- 1 whole brie, good quality
- 1 small onion, chopped
- 1 handful walnuts
- 1 handful almonds
- 4 pecans
- 1 tablespoon dried cranberries or diced apricots
- 1 teaspoon currants
- 1 tablespoon honey
- 1 teaspoon fresh thyme leaves

Direction

- Roast the walnuts, pecans and almonds in the oven or in a pan. Chop them coarsely and set aside
- Melt some butter in a pan and glaze the onion. Add the dried fruits and nuts. Add about 3-4 tablespoons of water, just to moisten the mixture a little. Now add the honey and thyme and stir some more.
- Slice the brie in two, widthwise. Place the nut-dried fruits mixture in between, just like a sandwich. You can serve it this way and add some arugula in the middle.
- OR you can bake the brie for about 10 minutes in the oven (350F).

23. Brie With Cherry Chipotle Chutney

Serving: Makes about 2 cups | Prep: | Cook: | Ready in:

Ingredients

- 1/2 tablespoon canola or vegetable oil
- 1/2 onion, finely diced
- 2 1/2 cups cherries, pitted, quartered (including juice)
- 1/2 teaspoon coriander seeds, lightly toasted, crushed
- 1 chipotle in adobo, seeds removed and chopped (be careful to avoid touching eyes or nose after handling seeds – they will burn)
- 1/4 cup cider vinegar
- 1/2 cup brown sugar
- Pinch ground cloves
- 1/4 cup slivered almonds, toasted
- 1 round of Brie (6-8 oz)

Direction

- Heat oil in small saucepan over medium-hi heat.
- Add onions and coriander seeds and cook until onions begin to soften, about 2 minutes.
- Add cherries with juice, chipotle, vinegar, sugar and cloves. Bring to boil and then reduce heat, simmering uncovered for about 30 minutes.
- Stir in almond slivers. Take off heat and allow mixture to cool.
- If making ahead of time, transfer to glass jars with lids (either two ½-pint jars or one 1-pint jar). Refrigerate until ready to use.
- Preheat broiler.
- Trim off white rind from top of brie, being careful not to waste too much cheese.
- Place trimmed brie in broiler safe dish. Score top of brie lightly, to allow chutney juices to seep into cheese.
- Spoon desired amount of chutney on top of brie. (For a 6 oz. round, I used 4 generous teaspoons).
- Broil for 5-7 minutes, checking to make sure almonds do not burn.
- Place on serving plate and enjoy.

24. Brioche Circles With Brie And Cherries

Serving: Makes 8 circles | Prep: | Cook: | Ready in:

Ingredients

- Brioche dough
- 2 1/4 cups (315 g) all-purpose flour
- 2 1/4 cups (340 g) bread flour
- 3 1/4 teaspoons active dry yeast
- 1/3 cup 1 Tbs. (80 g) sugar
- 1 tablespoon kosher salt
- 5 large eggs
- 1 cup 6 Tbs. (310 g) unsalted butter, at room temp, cut into about a dozen pieces
- Filling and assembly
- 3 1/2 cups (About) ripe cherries, washed, stemmed, and pitted
- 3 tablespoons honey
- 8 pieces of Brie, each about 1 or 1.5-inch square and about 1/3-inch thick
- 1/2 the batch of brioche dough

Direction

- Brioche dough
- Combine the flours, yeast, sugar, salt, eggs, and 120 ml (1/2 cup) of room temp. water in the bowl of a standing mixer with a dough hook and mix until combined, scraping down the sides of the bowl as necessary. Once the ingredients have come together, mix on low speed for about 3 more minutes. The dough will seem very dry, it has to be because you're going to be adding a whole lot of butter!
- Still mixing on low speed, add the butter one piece at a time, adding each new piece only after the previous piece has gotten fully mixed in and has disappeared into the dough. This will take a while and as you add more butter, the dough will start to smell marvelously like cake batter. Once all the butter has been added, scrape the sides of the bowl down then mix for 10 more minutes.
- At this point, give your mixer a 5 minute break to let its motor cool down just a little. Then, turn it up to medium speed and beat the dough until it becomes soft and a bit shiny, about 10 or 15 minutes. At first as you start to beat it will look like there's no hope for the dough, like it's just a shaggy mess, but give it time and it will become smooth and silky as the mixer does its work. Once the dough starts to look smooth and silky, turn the mixer to medium-high and beat for 1 more minute (the dough should make a slightly uncomfortable thwapping and slapping sound as it hits the sides of the bowl). Turn the mixer off and test the dough by pinching a little of it between your fingers and pulling it gently outward. It should stretch a bit towards you. If it breaks

- immediately, mix the dough for 2-3 more minutes.
- Transfer the dough in a big ball to a large bowl and cover it with plastic wrap, gently laying the plastic directly atop the surface of the dough. Put the dough into the refrigerator to proof overnight, or at least 6 hours. During this time it will only rise a little bit.
- Remove from the fridge when ready to use. The brioche circles require only half of this dough. The remaining half can be frozen for a week then thawed overnight in the fridge to make more goodies next week! You can also bake the second half into a brioche loaf (good for sandwiches) by shaping it and placing it in a loaf pan to rise for 4 hours, then baking at 350F until deeply golden, about 35 minutes.
- Filling and assembly
- To prepare the cherries, combine the whole pitted cherries with the honey in a heavy bottomed saucepan. Cook over medium-high heat until they start to bubble, then turn the heat to low and cook, covered, for 10 minutes, until the cherries are soft and soupy. Allow to cool completely. (This can be done the night before baking when you have to make the brioche dough anyway.)
- To make the brioche circles, divide the half-batch of brioche dough into 8 equal pieces. Flatten each piece and stretch each into a circle about 4 or 5 inches across. They should be very thin in the middle with a thicker rim, like making tiny pizzas.
- Line two rimmed baking sheets with parchment paper and put 4 of the circles on each. Let the brioche circles rest at room temperature for 30 minutes to soften and puff just slightly. In the meantime, heat your oven to 350F.
- Put a piece of brie in the center of each of the circles, then top the brie with a large spoonful of cherries and just a very small amount of the cherry juices. Each circle should get about 5 or 6 cherries. (Save the leftover cherry juice to mix into drinks – think a splash of cherry juice, a splash of bourbon, a squirt of lemon juice, and soda…)

- Bake the brioches in the oven until they are golden brown and the filling is bubbling, about 25-30 minutes, being sure to switch the positions of the pans and rotate them halfway through the baking time.
- Allow the brioches to cool on the baking sheets for 10 minutes before transferring to a wire rack. Serve at least a few of them still warm (but not hot or, trust me, you will burn the heck out of your mouth) from the oven accompanied by cups of strong coffee, since they are definitely the most magical while fresh. Wrap any leftovers tightly and keep them in the refrigerator for up to 3 days. Rewarm them gently in the oven or a toaster oven (about 8 minutes at 325F) before eating.

25. Buckwheat Crepes With Brie + Honey Sauteed Swiss Chard

Serving: Serves 4 | Prep: | Cook: | Ready in:

Ingredients

- 1/2 cup buckwheat or all-purpose flour
- 2/3 cup milk
- 2 large eggs
- 3 tablespoons melted salted butter, divided
- Kosher salt and freshly ground black pepper
- 8 ounces brie, thinly sliced
- 2 bunches Swiss chard, leaves sliced into 2-inch pieces
- 2 teaspoons honey
- 2 teaspoons red-wine vinegar

Direction

- Combine milk, eggs, 1 tablespoon butter, 1/2 teaspoon salt and flour in a blender; blend to combine (about 1 minute).
- Meanwhile, heat large nonstick skillet over medium-high. Wipe skillet with a lightly greased paper towel. Add enough batter to thinly coat bottom of skillet, swirling pan while pouring (about 1/4 cup batter). Cook

crepe until lightly golden, about 2 minutes; flip and cook 1 minute more. Transfer cooked crepe to a plate and cover with a clean kitchen towel. Repeat with remaining batter and stack crepes as they are cooked.
- While crepes cook, heat remaining 1 tablespoon butter in a separate medium skillet over medium heat. Add chard, season with salt and pepper, and cook, tossing, until endive is tender, about 5 minutes. Stir in honey and vinegar.
- To assemble crepes, fold each crepe in half. Arrange brie slices on crepes, then top with sautéed chard. Fold crepes into thirds and serve.

26. Caramelized Apple Tart With Brie Puff Pastry (Tarte Tatin)

Serving: Makes one 10-inch tart | Prep: | Cook: | Ready in:

Ingredients

- Brie Puff Pastry
- 1 cup unsalted butter, COLD (cut into 8 pieces)
- 2 cups organic unbleached flour
- 4 ounces French Brie cheese, at room temperature [You want a fresh one with a light crust.]
- Apple Filling
- 6 crisp apples (Golden Delicious or Gala are the most like French apples)
- 1/3 cup organic cane sugar
- 1 teaspoon ground cinnamon (I like Vann's Saigon Cinnamon)
- 2 tablespoons unsalted butter, softened
- 1/2 cup organic dark brown cane sugar
- 6 tablespoons melted butter

Direction

- In food processor fitted with the metal blade, combine the flour and butter with short pulses until mixture is the consistency of coarse meal.
- Cut the Brie into several small pieces and add to the flour mixture. Pulse until just before mixture forms a ball. Form mixture into a disc and refrigerate for at least ½ hour.
- Apple Filling
- Quarter, core and peel apples. Cut them lengthwise into 1/8-inch slices (thin). Mix cinnamon and sugar and toss with the apples.
- Butter a 10-inch ovenproof deep fry pie pan heavily with the 2 tablespoons soft butter. Make sure you coat the bottom especially well. Sprinkle half of the 1/2 cup of sugar over the butter. Arrange 1/3 of the apples over the sugar. Sprinkle 1/3 of the melted butter over the apples. Repeat with 1/2 the remaining apples and butter, then a final layer of apples and butter. Put remaining sugar on top. Cook on top of the stove (over medium-low heat) for about 20 minutes, until apples have softened and begun to caramelize.
- Heat oven to 350 degrees F. Roll out pastry to 1/8-inch thick. Cut it into a circle the size of the top of the pie pan. Place over the apples, letting the edges fall against the inside edge of the dish. Cut 4 or 5 holes about 1/8-inch long in pastry as vents.
- Bake in lower third of preheated oven for 45 to 60 minutes. If pastry is browning too fast, cover lightly with aluminum foil. Tart is done when you can see thick brown syrup exuding from apples between the crust and edge of pan.

27. Caramelized Pear And Melted Brie On Brioche

Serving: Makes about 16 triangles | Prep: | Cook: | Ready in:

Ingredients

- 1 loaf brioche, cut into 1/2 inch slices

- 2 ripe, but slightly firm, pears
- 1 tablespoon butter
- 8 ounces brie
- 1 tablespoon extra virgin olive oil, plus more as needed
- Juice of one lemon
- Maldon salt or other finishing salt, to taste
- Freshly cracked black pepper, to taste

Direction

- Preheat your oven to 350°F.
- Cut the sliced brioche in half to make triangular wedges and line them up on a parchment-lined baking sheet. Bake until toasted but not too toasty, about 6 minutes.
- Cut the pears in half. Scoop out the core and any tough surrounding flesh. Slice the pears to about 1/4 inch thick. Heat the butter in a non-stick skillet to medium-high heat. Mix in the olive oil. Place the pear slices in the pan, making sure not to crowd them. Sear until caramelized, about 3 minutes.
- Spread a generous covering of brie on your brioche slices. Top with 1 to 2 pear slices, caramelized side up. At this point, you can opt to broil the assembled toasts just long enough to melt the brie or leave as is.
- Drizzle the finished toasts with a few drops of lemon juice. Top with a couple flakes of Maldon and some freshly cracked black pepper.

28. Cavatappi With Sun Dried Tomatoes, Brie & Arugula

Serving: Serves 4 to 8 | Prep: | Cook: | Ready in:

Ingredients

- 12 ounces Brie, chopped
- 1 cup drained, oil-packed sun-dried tomatoes
- 2 large garlic cloves, minced or Microplaned
- 5 tablespoons extra-virgin olive oil
- Kosher salt
- Red pepper flakes
- 1 pound cavatappi
- 3 cups baby arugula

Direction

- Combine the Brie, sun-dried tomatoes, garlic, and olive oil in a large, heatproof bowl—this will become your serving bowl. Season with a big pinch each of salt and red pepper flakes (we'll adjust to taste more later, after the pasta arrives).
- Set a large pot of water over high heat. Add a few spoonful of kosher salt and bring to a boil. Cook the cavatappi for 8 to 9 minutes, until al dente. Before you drain the pasta, fill a mug or glass with the salty pasta water. Now you can drain.
- Add the just-drained pasta to the bowl with the Brie and sun-dried tomato mixture. Give a quick toss with a big spoon (don't use a fork, it will spear the noodles). Add the arugula and ¼ cup pasta water and keep tossing. Continue to add pasta water until the consistency and creaminess looks right to you—I used about ½ cup—and keep in mind that it will stiffen as it cools. Season with salt and red pepper flakes to taste. Serve immediately.

29. Cheese Plate

Serving: Serves a small group | Prep: | Cook: | Ready in:

Ingredients

- 8 figs - sliced
- 1 wedge of Brie - cut them in thick slices
- 1/3 cup honey

Direction

- Pre-heat the oven to 350 F.
- Place sliced figs in a baking dish and put them in the oven. Bake for about 10-15 minutes or until the figs get soft.

- For easy clean-up, place sliced Brie on parchment paper then carefully place the warm figs on the cheese and drizzled honey.
- The warm figs softened the Brie just enough without melting it. I served the figs & cheese with whole wheat toasts and French baguette slices. I also added some almonds, dark chocolate and of course, red grapes to the plate.

30. Cranberry Brie Crescent Wreath

Serving: Serves 8-10 | Prep: | Cook: | Ready in:

Ingredients

- CRANBERRY BRIE CRESCENT WREATH
- Pillsbury Original Crescent Rolls Twin Pack 8 oz
- 2 cups fresh cranberries
- 1 stem of rosemary
- 1/2 cup apple cider
- 1 8 ounces wheel of brie
- spiced pecans (recipe below)
- additional cranberries and rosemary to garnish
- Spiced Pecans
- 1/2 teaspoon kosher salt
- 1/4 teaspoon cayenne pepper
- 1/4 teaspoon ground cinnamon
- 1/4 teaspoon ground allspice
- 1/4 teaspoon ground cardamom
- 1/2 teaspoon smoked paprika
- 1/2 pound pecan halves
- 2 tablespoons 2 tablespoons unsalted
- 3 tablespoons packed dark brown sugar
- 1 1/2 tablespoons water

Direction

- CRANBERRY BRIE CRESCENT WREATH
- Begin by making the cranberry sauce. In a medium sized saucepan over medium heat, dissolve the sugar in the apple cider. Stir in the cranberries and stem of rosemary and cook until the cranberries start to pop (about 10 minutes). Remove from heat and place sauce in a bowl, discard the rosemary stem. Allow to thicken and cool at room temperature before assembling your wreath.
- Preheat oven to 350 degrees Fahrenheit.
- Open your twin pack of Pillsbury Original Crescent Rolls and roll them out on a cutting board. Press together the perforations of the rolls to create a solid sheet of dough.
- Split the cranberry sauce between the two sheets of dough and gently spread all over, leaving a square at the bottom for the cheese.
- Using a pizza cutter, cut out 1-inch lengthwise strips of the crescent dough.
- Remove your brie from the package and trim off the top and bottom rind. Cut into 1-inch squares (they don't have to be perfect).
- Place one square of brie on the exposed portion of the crescent dough and roll towards the other side, keeping it as tight as possible like you're making a cinnamon roll. Repeat for all of the strips.
- Place the rolls on a parchment or Silpat-lined baking sheet in the shape of a wreath. You can either do one giant one (it may take a few minutes longer to bake) or two smaller ones. I chose to make two.
- Bake in the preheated oven for 12-15 minutes until golden brown and bubbly.
- While the wreath is still warm, top each roll with a spiced pecan.
- Decorate with additional cranberries and rosemary for a festive centerpiece!
- Spiced Pecans
- Line a clean counter or baking sheet with a piece of parchment paper or foil.
- Mix the spices together in a small bowl and set aside.
- Stir in the spices until just fragrant (15-30 seconds) then add the butter pats and stir to melt. Follow that with the sugar. When thoroughly mixed add the water. Stir 2 to 3 minutes or until the sugar has completely and the nuts look glazed. Sprinkle over with the kosher salt and remove from heat.

- Spread the nuts evenly onto the parchment or foil so that they don't dry in clumps. Cool completely before transferring to an airtight container for storage at room temp for up to three weeks.

31. Cranberry Brie Puff Pastries

Serving: Makes 24 puffs. | Prep: | Cook: | Ready in:

Ingredients

- for the cranberry jam
- 2 cups fresh cranberries
- 1 cup granulated sugar
- 1 teaspoon lime zest (or any other citrus zest)
- 2-3 teaspoons lime juice (or any other juice)
- 1 pinch salt
- 1/2 teaspoon ground cinnamon (optional)
- 1-2 teaspoons cornstarch (optional)
- for the puff pastry, and everything else
- 2 cups all-purpose flour
- 1/2 teaspoon table salt
- 1 teaspoon sugar
- 1 1/4 cups (2 1/2 sticks) unsalted butter, very cold, cut into 1/2-inch pieces
- 6 to 8 tablespoons ice water
- 1 egg yolk, for brushing and sealing
- 1 teaspoon water or milk
- 4-6 ounces brie

Direction

- To make the cranberry jam, combine cranberries, sugar, lime zest, lime juice, salt, and cinnamon in a small pot over medium-high heat. (I know, it seemed crazy to me that there was so little liquid. But it's magic.) Stir the mixture continuously as it heats; after a few minutes, the sugar will become liquid, and after a few more, the cranberries will begin to pop.
- When the mixture is fully liquid, turn the heat down to low and let it simmer for around ten to fifteen more minutes. A few minutes before removing from the heat, you can add a sprinkle of cornstarch to aid in setting the jam, but it's not really necessary. (I also didn't find the need to create a slurry beforehand.) Pour into a clean jar and let cool before chilling in the refrigerator.
- To make the pastry, first whisk together flour, salt, and sugar in a large bowl. Add the butter pieces and mix again briefly, just to distribute throughout. Next, add 6 tablespoons water (best to try to sprinkle it over the entire mixture) and mix with a fork just until the dough comes together, as gently as possible. It's fine and preferable to keep chunks of butter intact — it will add to the flakiness. If you're seeing a lot of loose flour after mixing for a while, add a little more water, one tablespoon at a time. (KAF also recommends spritzing with a water spray bottle if you have one.) But work with it a little and see if it doesn't come together first.
- When it's holding together, turn the mixture out onto a work surface and shape into a rectangle about the size of a piece of paper, with the short side facing you. Fold dough into thirds like a letter — bottom third up, then top third over the bottom third. Rotate the dough, so that the short side faces you again, and fold into a letter again. Lightly flour the surface as necessary, then rotate to the short side one more time and fold again. Wrap with plastic and refrigerate for at least 30 minutes.
- After the dough has rested, fold into letters three more times, wrap, and refrigerate for at least one more hour. After this, you're ready to roll the dough out and cut it into rounds for use. I divided the dough into two balls and rolled each into squares that were about 12" to 16" across. Using a cookie cutter, biscuit cutter, or just a regular drinking glass, cut the dough into circles. My batch yielded about 48 rounds. The dough will likely have softened by this point — I placed them in a single layer onto saran wrap, place another piece of saran wrap over that, and refrigerated them again until firm.

- Finally, preheat the oven to 375 degrees. Whisk the egg yolk and a splash of water together to make the egg wash. For each puff, lay out one round and brush it with egg wash — this will help seal the puff shut. Place a slice of brie and a dollop of cranberry jam on the bottom round. Take another round and stretch it a bit between your fingers (it needs to be a bit bigger to fit over the filling) and place it on top. Crimp the edges shut with the tines of a fork, brush egg wash over the top, and prick the puff in the center to ventilate.
- Place the sealed rounds on a parchment-lined baking sheet — they can be as close together as you like, since they will not spread (just puff!) Bake at 375 degrees for 12-14 minutes or until golden brown on top. Let cool slightly, and serve! They're delicious warm or room temperature.

32. Cranberry Chipotle Marmalade

Serving: Serves 12-14 | Prep: | Cook: | Ready in:

Ingredients

- 12 ounces Fresh Cranberries
- 1/3 cup Dried Currants
- 3/4 cup Light Brown Sugar
- 1/3 cup Water
- 1/4 teaspoon Cinnamon
- 3 (more or less) tablespoons Canned Chipotles, Pureed
- 1 pinch Salt
- 2 8 oz. Wheels of Brie

Direction

- Put cranberries, currants, brown sugar, and water in a large saucepan. Meanwhile, puree chipotle. Scrape off the adobo sauce, and depending on how hot you like things, remove seeds and adjust amount of chipotle you actually use. I use my Cuisinart to puree, but you could easily do a very fine chop on these. Once berries begin to pop, add chipotle, cinnamon and salt. Once berries have all popped, allow to cool. At this point, you can refrigerate it for later use.
- When you are ready to serve, pour marmalade over wheels of brie and bake in a 350 oven until brie is softened (about 20 minutes).
- I like this best served with warmed tostadas.
- If you would rather not use the brie, you can easily substitute blocks of cream cheese.

33. Cream Of Brie Soup

Serving: Serves 6 | Prep: | Cook: | Ready in:

Ingredients

- 1/4c chopped onion
- 1 med. Leek[white part only] chopped
- 1/2c thinly sliced celery
- 4tbs unsalted butter
- 1/4c flour
- 2c whole milk
- 2c home made chicken broth
- 3/4lb Brie cubed[1/2lb 60%fat brie de Paris+1/4lb herb brie]
- Pinch cayenne
- Salt & Pepper to taste
- Chopped chives for garnish

Direction

- In a 3qt. kettle, sauté the onion, leek & celery in the butter until limp.
- Stir in the flour, remove from heat, stir in the milk & chicken broth using a whisk to mix well.
- Return to heat & simmer stirring constantly until soup thickens.
- Add all the Brie [with the rind on] and stir until melted.
- Run all of this through a food processor until very smooth.
- Correct seasoning with S&P and cayenne serve hot with garnish.

34. Creamy Avocado And Brie Sandwich

Serving: Serves 2 | Prep: | Cook: | Ready in:

Ingredients

- 4 slices of bread
- 1/2 piece ripe avocado, pitted and peeled
- 3 to 4 ounces brie cheese
- 1/2 tablespoon spreadable butter
- 2 tablespoons dijonnaise

Direction

- Slice brie. Cut avocado in half and slice thinly. Spread each bread with butter followed by dijonnaise. Place sliced avocado and brie on two slices of bread, then make sandwiches with two remaining bread. Cut each sandwich in half.
- Serve with vegetarian antipasto such as marinated sun dried tomatoes and olives.

35. Croissants Filled With Brie & Strawberries

Serving: Serves 1 | Prep: | Cook: | Ready in:

Ingredients

- 1 croissant
- flavorful lettuce, such as Red Salanova, washed & dried
- brie, sliced
- strawberries, washed, hulled, & sliced

Direction

- Using a serrated knife, cut the croissants in half horizontally without cutting all the way through. We want to make a kind of pocket for our fillings. Fill the croissants with lettuce, brie, and sliced strawberries. Honestly, it is impossible to overload them with strawberries so be generous with them.
- Enjoy with a cup of coffee (either warm or iced) or a glass of freshly squeezed juice. Et voilà!

36. Dan Rooney's Signature Burger

Serving: Serves 1 | Prep: | Cook: | Ready in:

Ingredients

- For Burger
- 1/4 bunch watercress
- 1 ounce brie cheese
- 2 ounces honey peppercorn aioli
- 1 ounce red onions
- 1 potato roll
- 8 ounces burger patty
- For Honey Peppercorn Aioli
- 3 cups mayonnaise
- 1/4 pure honey
- 2 ounces thyme, freshly chopped
- 2 ounces rosemary, freshly chopped
- 4 ounces shallots, peeled
- 1/2 roast garlic, pureed
- 1 lemon, freshly squeezed
- 2 ounces black peppercorn, crushed

Direction

- Grill burger, place on bun, top with Brie cheese, onions and watercress. Spread aioli sauce on inside of bun top and place on top of the burger.

37. Duck Confit, Pear, And Fennel Bites

Serving: Makes 24 bites | Prep: | Cook: | Ready in:

Ingredients

- 1 sheet puff pastry - defrosted
- 1 duck leg confit - skin removed, meat chopped
- 1 small bulb fennel, chopped
- 1 large firm pear, peeled and chopped
- 1 teaspoon thyme leaves, minced
- 1 clove garlic, minced
- 1 tablespoon olive oil
- 5 ounces brie cheese, rinds included, chopped into 1/2 inch pieces
- 1 tablespoon sherry vinegar

Direction

- Mix on a baking sheet the fennel, pear, thyme, garlic, and olive oil, and season with salt and pepper. Roast for 30 minutes in a 400 degree, preheated oven. Stir 2-3 times. Remove.
- Add chopped duck confit and sherry vinegar to hot cookie sheet. Stir to combine. Taste and season again with salt and pepper if necessary.
- Roll out your thawed puff pastry on a floured work surface to a 12 inch square. Cut the puff pastry sheet into 24 equal pieces. Press each piece into a mini-muffin tin (you'll need more than 1 muffin tin), making a small cup.
- Place 1 square brie cheese in each mini-muffin cup. Add 1.5 teaspoons of the duck, sherry, pear, fennel mixture. Bake in a pre-heated 375 degree oven for 25 minutes. Let cool 5 minutes before serving. Garnish with fresh thyme leaves if desired.

38. Dutch Mustard Soup

Serving: Serves 6-8 | Prep: | Cook: | Ready in:

Ingredients

- 2 tablespoons Butter
- 4 cups Mustard greens, trimmed and stems removed
- 2 Leeks, sliced into thin rings
- 2 Garlic cloves peeled and smashed
- 5 cups Veggie stock
- 1 cup Dark beer
- 3 tablespoons Mustard, I used Grey Poupon Dijon
- 8 ounces Brie soft cheese rind trimmed and cubed
- Pinch Salt and White pepper, to taste

Direction

- In a Dutch oven over medium heat melt the butter. Add the leeks, garlic and a pinch of salt cook for 12-15 minutes until leeks are tender and light brown. Add the cup of beer to deglaze all the good bits off the bottom of the pan. Next into the pot all the greens and the stock. Bring to a slow boil and cover. Cook down the greens until tender about 7-10 minutes. Take pot off the heat. Using an immersion blender puree the greens until smooth. Be very careful not to splash it's going to be very hot!
- Once the greens are smooth return the pot back to medium heat and cook until it just starts to bubble. Stir in the mustard and the cubes of Brie until the cheese has melted and the soup has thickened. Season with more salt and white pepper to taste. Enjoy!

39. Em's Buns

Serving: Makes 2-dozen buns | Prep: | Cook: | Ready in:

Ingredients

- Bun dough
- 1 1/2 cups good quality whole milk
- 6 tablespoons un salted butter, melted
- 2 teaspoons raw cane sugar
- 1 tablespoon active dry yeast
- 2 eggs, lightly beaten
- 1 egg yolk, lightly beaten (save the white for the egg wash)
- 1 teaspoon sea salt

- 5 cups about, all purpose flour (plus more as needed)
- Bun filling
- 6 ounces provolone cheese, cut into 12 small cubes
- 6-7 ounces good quality hard salami, chopped
- 1/2 cup chopped, pitted green olives
- 6 ounces good brie (or another similar triple creme cheese)- rind removed and cut into 12 pieces (this is easier if it is cold)
- 1 cup finely chopped strawberries
- 1 tablespoon granulated sugar
- 1 tablespoon finely chopped fresh mint
- 1 egg white for egg wash
- sesame seeds for sprinkling
- pearl sugar for sprinkling

Direction

- Bun dough
- Heat the milk to just over 100F, then in a large bowl, stir together the warm milk, melted butter, sugar, and yeast. Let this stand for about 5 minutes, until the yeast is foamy.
- Stir in the 2 eggs, egg yolk, and salt. Then stir in about 4-4 1/2 cups of the flour and mix well with a wooden spoon. (This can all be done in the bowl of a standing mixer using a bread hook as well). At this point you should have a shaggy dough that pulls away from the sides of the bowl.
- Turn the dough out onto a floured surface (use the last 1/2 cup of flour) and knead, adding more flour in small amounts if needed (ooh, pun!), for about 10 minutes, until the dough is elastic and smooth. If you're mixing the dough in a mixer, add a bit of the extra flour (about 1/4-1/2 cup), just enough to give you a stiff dough and mix on low with the bread hook for 10 minutes.
- Coat a deep bowl with a little bit of oil, put the dough into the bowl, turn the dough to lightly coat it with oil, then cover the bowl with plastic wrap and stick it in the refrigerator overnight.
- After about 12 hours, punch down the dough, then fill and bake it as directed below.
- Bun filling
- First off, toss the strawberries with the sugar and mint and set aside.
- Take the dough out of the refrigerator, punch it down, and divide it in half. Put half back in the fridge. Roll the half you have out into a log, then divide this log into 12 equal pieces (I usually divide it in half, then half again, then thirds, but if I were really being detail oriented I would use a scale).
- One at a time, take a piece and roll it into a ball. Stretch this ball into a circle about a quarter inch thick, and pull it even thinner around the edges.
- In the middle of the dough circle, place one piece of provolone, a couple little pieces of salami (1/12th of the salami pieces, in fact), and a small scoop of the chopped olives. Then, take the edges of the circle and gather them up around the filling, pinching and twisting them tightly together to close up the bun. Place on a parchment lined baking sheet.
- Repeat this procedure with the remaining 11 pieces that you cut filling them with the provolone, salami, olive mix. Once this dozen are on the baking sheet, cover with a kitchen towel and set aside to rise for 30 minutes.
- Then, start the second dozen. Take the remaining dough out of the fridge and divide it into 12 pieces.
- Fill these buns in the same manner as the first, except put a piece of brie and a scoop of the strawberries in each. Put these buns on a second parchment lined baking sheet. When finished, cover with a clean towel and set aside to rise for 30 minutes.
- Preheat the oven to 350F. When the first dozen buns have finished rising, brush them with the egg white and sprinkle them with a pinch of sesame seeds each. Bake for 20 minutes, or until golden and cooked through. Transfer to a cooling rack immediately.
- In the meantime, brush the second dozen buns with the egg wash and sprinkle them with a pinch of pearl sugar each. When the first batch is baked, bake the second batch.

- The buns are the very best still slightly warm from the oven, and are definitely best the day they are baked. But, they keep for a couple of days and rewarm nicely. (And of course, they're especially good sold out of a special food stand trailer attached to a bike parked on a street corner...I imagine.)

40. Fiesta Bruschetta

Serving: Makes 12 pieces | Prep: | Cook: | Ready in:

Ingredients

- 1 cup seeds from 1 large pomegranate
- 1 French baguette
- 2 cloves garlic sliced
- 2 tablespoons olive oil
- 4 ounces soft-ripened brie cheese (recommended: goat brie)
- 1 cup apricot preserves
- Rosemary sprig for garnish

Direction

- Break open the pomegranate under water to free the seeds. The seeds will sink to the bottom of the bowl and the rest will float to the top. Discard the white membrane and put the seeds in a separate bowl. Reserve 1 cup of the seeds and set aside.
- Preheat oven to 400°F.
- Place garlic slices in olive oil and microwave for 1 minute to infuse the olive oil with garlic. Cut the baguette into 1/2-inch slices. Brush olive oil on one side of baguette slices. Lay bread on a baking sheet and place in the preheated oven. Bake for 5 to 6 minutes. (The bread does not need to brown, just have a toast-like crust on the top surface.)
- Spread apricot preserves on toasted bread.
- Microwave brie cheese for 10-15 seconds to soften the cheese. Cut the brie in half and spoon or drizzle the cheese on the toasted bread.
- Place a teaspoon of pomegranate seeds on each slice.
- Serve while warm.

41. Fig, Brie & Prosciutto Pizza

Serving: Serves 8 | Prep: | Cook: | Ready in:

Ingredients

- 6 Black mission figs, sliced into quarters
- 4 teaspoons balsamic vinegar, divided
- 1 ball prepared pizza dough
- 3 tablespoons extra virgin olive oil, divided
- 8 ounces Brie cheese, sliced
- 2 ounces prosciutto, sliced
- 2 ounces baby arugula leaves
- Kosher salt
- Freshly ground black pepper

Direction

- Preheat oven to 450.
- Toss the quartered figs with 2 teaspoons of balsamic vinegar in a small bowl. Set aside.
- Stretch the pizza dough out on a baking sheet and shape into a rectangle approximately 9x12 inches or until the crust is ½-inch thick. Brush the surface with 1 tablespoon of olive oil. Arrange the brie slices evenly over the pizza. Bake 12-15 minutes until dough is golden and cheese is melted. Remove pizza from oven and place the quartered figs on top. Return pizza to oven for an additional 5 minutes until figs are slightly softened. Remove from heat. Arrange prosciutto slices evenly over the pizza.
- Whisk the remaining 2 teaspoons of balsamic vinegar and 2 tablespoons of olive oil together in a medium bowl. Toss the dressing with the baby arugula leaves. Season with salt and pepper to taste. Arrange the baby arugula on top of the pizza. Cut into slices and serve warm.

42. Fig, Prosciutto And Brie Puffs

Serving: Serves 15-20 people | Prep: | Cook: | Ready in:

Ingredients

- 1 packet Of Frozen Phyllo Dough
- 1/4 pound Thinly Sliced Prosciutto
- 1 French Brie Cheese Wedge
- 1/4 cup Cooked Sweet Onions
- 1 Container of your favorite Fig Fruit Paste or Jam
- 4-5 tablespoons Of Melted Butter

Direction

- Reheat your oven to 350 degrees. Cook your onions in butter just till their translucent – drain them on a paper towel. Cut your phyllo dough into 2×2 inch squares (approximately). Cut your fruit paste, prosciutto and brie in about 1 inch sizes.
- Stack your brie and fruit paste and layer of onion mixture, wrap the prosciutto around to create a 'bag' to hold the ingredients, then place your mixture in the middle of your phyllo dough (make sure you have 2-3 sheets layered).
- You can simply fold them or if you'd like to create the 'purse like' shapes I did simply pinch the extra dough at the top. Make sure all the seams are covered with dough they don't have to be perfect more than likely some fig will spill through. Brush your puffs with your melted butter. Bakes for about 10 minutes or until golden.

43. Flamiche Au Maroilles Avec Pêche

Serving: Makes one 6 inch tart | Prep: | Cook: | Ready in:

Ingredients

- 1 small sage leaf (or other herb of your choice such as rosemary or thyme)
- 1 small pat of butter, unsalted
- 1 small peach, peeled, sliced and lightly salted with kosher salt
- wedge of lemon, Meyer if you have it
- 4 ounces of dough (challah or brioche), puff pastry or pâte brisée pastry crust
- 1 ounce of brie (or comparable cheese)
- 1 egg
- 2 ounces crème fraîche (or quark)
- pinch of Maldon salt flakes or kosher salt
- pinch of crushed pink and white peppercorns
- dash of sweet Hungarian paprika

Direction

- Let the peach slices rest with the salt for about 10 minutes. Roll and finely snip a small sage leaf to a chiffonade. Heat and brown the butter in a small pan. Add the sage leaf and the sliced peaches; cook for 1 minute or less. Take off heat. Squeeze some lemon juice on the peaches and set aside.
- Roll out the dough to fit a 6 inch tart pan.
- Cut the brie into half inch cubes and place them across the bottom of the tart shell. Add the peaches (without the sage).
- Whisk the crème fraîche with the egg. Pour this over the brie and peaches. Sprinkle the salt, pepper, and paprika on top.
- Bake for about 25 minutes in a preheated 375 degree oven or until golden brown. Let cool and serve warm. If you like, top with the fried sage (or rosemary or thyme).

44. French Toast With Pears, Blood Orange Caramel Sauce, And Brie

Serving: Serves 6 | Prep: | Cook: | Ready in:

Ingredients

- Roasted Pears and Brie
- 2 bosc pears (sliced into about 8 long pieces)
- 3 tablespoons EVOO
- 1 tablespoon coarse ground sea salt
- 1/2 wheel of brie
- French Toast and Caramel Sauce
- 6 slices baguette
- 2 eggs
- 1/2 cup half and half
- 1 teaspoon cinnamon
- 3 tablespoons butter (divided by tbsp)
- 1 cup sugar
- 1/4 cup water
- 1 teaspoon vanilla extract
- 1 blood orange (cut in half - half for juice, half for garnish)

Direction

- Roasted Pears and Brie
- 1. Preheat oven to 425 degrees. On a lightly greased baking sheet, spread pear slices, pour EVOO and sea salt over the top. Cook for approx. 5 minutes each side.
- Reduce heat to 375. Bake brie wheel for about 10 minutes or until it is slightly runny.
- French Toast and Caramel Sauce
- In a mixing bowl, whisk eggs, half and half, and cinnamon. Place bread slices in mixture and toss to coat.
- Heat 1st tbsp. butter in a skillet on medium high. Fry 2 pieces of bread for about 2 minutes each side, or until lightly browned. Set each piece on its own plate. Repeat twice with remaining bread and butter.
- Mix sugar and water and vanilla, heat on medium high in thick bottom sauce pan, stirring occasionally. Once it turns a nice caramel color, stir in blood orange juice, stirring quickly, and remove pan from heat.
- Each plate should start with piece of French toast, top with pears, drizzle with caramel sauce. Serve with a small slice of brie and an orange slice.

45. French Baguette Sandwich

Serving: Serves 2 | Prep: | Cook: | Ready in:

Ingredients

- 1 baguette
- 3 leeks
- brie
- 2 tablespoons brown sugar
- 1 teaspoon butter
- salt and pepper

Direction

- Start by caramelizing the leeks. Add the butter in the pan to melt and then add the leeks with the brown sugar on low heat and stir. When they turn transparent and brown (but not burnt) they will be ready.
- Add some salt and pepper at the end.
- Cut the baguette lengthwise and fill it with the caramelized leeks, the brie and the beetroots in this order.

46. Fusilli With Fresh Heirloom Tomatoes And Brie

Serving: Serves 4 | Prep: | Cook: | Ready in:

Ingredients

- 1 pound dried fusilli
- 1 wedge of triple creme brie at room temperature
- juice and zest of 1 small lemon
- 6-7 ripe Heirloom tomatoes
- 1/3 cup good olive oil
- 2-3 cloves garlic, minced
- 1 bunch fresh basil, coursely chopped
- 1 teaspoon salt
- fresh ground black pepper

Direction

- Bring a large pot of salted water to a boil. Cook pasta until al dente according to directions on package. Preheat the oven to warm.
- Slice half of the tomatoes in half and grate flesh side down using a box grater into a large serving bowl. Discard skins. Add garlic, salt, pepper, olive oil, lemon juice and lemon zest to bowl. Mix and place in warmed oven.
- Quarter the remaining tomatoes and remove the pulp. Cut quarters into bite-sized pieces. Set aside.
- Cut brie into 1/2 in cubes. Set aside.
- Add drained, cooked pasta, tomatoes, brie and basil to ingredients in bowl and toss. Serve immediately. Fresh grated parmesan can be a nice addition at the table.

47. Grape And Brie Barley Salad

Serving: Serves 4 to 6 as a side dish | Prep: | Cook: | Ready in:

Ingredients

- 1 cup pearl barley
- wedge brie - 4 to 5 ounces
- 1/3 cup plus 1 to 2 tablespoons mayonnaise
- 1 tablespoon extra virgin olive oil (a fruity one if you've got options)
- 1 tablespoon plus 1 teaspoon sherry vinegar
- 1/4 cup minced chives
- 1 to 1 1/2 teaspoons minced rosemary
- 1/2 teaspoon freshly ground black pepper
- 1/8 to 1/4 teaspoon fine sea salt
- bunch seedless red grapes (enough for 1 cup quartered)
- 1/2 cup chopped toasted walnuts

Direction

- Do ahead: Rinse barley and place in a 3 to 4 quart stock pot. Cover with 2 quarts water. Bring to a boil over high, then turn down to maintain a low simmer. Cook until soft but still a bit chewy, about 30 to 40 minutes. Drain the barley and transfer to a storage container. Allow to cool before covering and chilling. (If desired skim the foam and strain the water into a bowl to make lemon barley water.) You should have about 3 1/2 to 3 3/4 cups cooked barley. (NOTE: I didn't salt the water because I wanted to drink it. If you salt the cooking water, make sure to leave out the salt in the recipe until tasting it at the end.)
- When ready to make the salad: Place the brie in the freezer for 20 to 30 minutes to firm it up a bit so it is easier to cube.
- Combine the cooked barley, 1/3 cup mayonnaise, olive oil, sherry vinegar, chives, 1 teaspoon rosemary, black pepper, and 1/8 teaspoon salt in a medium bowl. Fold and stir until everything is well combined. If it seems dry, add another 1 to 2 tablespoons mayonnaise.
- Quarter enough grapes (pole to pole) to measure 1 cup. Add the grapes and chopped walnuts to the barley mixture.
- Cut the rind from the brie, then cube the brie so the pieces are similar in size to the grape slivers. Add the brie to the bowl. Mix well. (The brie will start to melt a bit with stirring. I like it to get pretty incorporated into the mixture, so stir quite a bit) Taste and add salt and rosemary as needed. Serve immediately or cover and refrigerate until ready to serve. Garnish with a cluster of grapes and a sprig of rosemary if desired.

48. Grilled Brie Sandwiches With Honey, Pistachio & Kale Pesto

Serving: Makes 4 sandwiches | Prep: 0hours15mins | Cook: 0hours7mins | Ready in:

Ingredients

- For the pesto
- 1 cup packed torn kale leaves
- 1/4 cup honey

- 1/3 cup shelled, roasted pistachios
- 1 1/2 teaspoons lemon juice
- 3/4 teaspoon kosher salt
- 1/2 teaspoon grated lemon zest
- 2 tablespoons extra-virgin olive oil
- 2 tablespoons chopped fresh basil
- For the sandwiches
- 1/2 cup prepared kale pesto (recipe above)
- 8 slices high-quality crusty white bread, such as French bread
- 4 ounces Brie
- 4 tablespoons salted butter, divided

Direction

- For the pesto
- Combine all ingredients in a food processor and blend very well until smooth. Taste and adjust salt as necessary.
- For the sandwiches
- Spread 2 tablespoons of pesto on 4 slices of bread; set aside.
- Slice the Brie and divide it evenly among the remaining 4 slices of bread.
- Put the pesto-covered bread, pesto side down, on each Brie-covered slice of bread.
- Heat a large skillet over medium heat and melt 2 tablespoons of butter in it. Add the sandwiches to the skillet.
- Cook the sandwiches until golden brown on one side, about 3 to 4 minutes.
- When ready to flip the sandwiches, transfer them to a plate and add the remaining 2 tablespoons butter to the skillet.
- Once the butter is melted, add the sandwiches back to the skillet with the un-grilled side facing down. Cook for an additional 3 minutes, until the cheese is fully melted and the bread is crisp and golden brown on each side.
- Remove from the skillet, cut each sandwich in half, and serve immediately.

49. Grilled Brie Topped With Slow Roasted Sunblushed Tomatoes

Serving: Serves 6-8 | Prep: | Cook: |Ready in:

Ingredients

- Ingredients
- 1/4 cup olive oil
- 1 tablespoon lemon zest, finely grated
- 2 cloves garlic, minced
- 1 teaspoon fresh chilies, minced
- 6 mini wheels or three 4.5 oz wheels of brie cheese, at room temperature
- 1 ciabatta loaf
- 2 large cloves garlic, peeled
- Sublushed tomatoes, recipe follows
- Sunblushed Tomatoes
- 1/2 pound fresh cherry tomatoes
- 1/2 teaspoon sea salt
- 1/4 teaspoon dried thyme
- 1/4 teaspoon dried oregano
- 1/4 cup olive oil

Direction

- Preheat barbecue to medium-high. Whisk the olive oil in a large bowl with the lemon zest, garlic and chilies. Add brie to the bowl and coat with the mixture. Let stand for 15 minutes.
- Slice the baguette, pide or ciabatta and toast pieces over medium-high on a barbecue grill rack. As they are done rub them, one at a time, with a whole garlic clove. Season with a little sea salt, then stack them one on top of the other and set aside.
- Arrange the cheeses on grill racks. Drizzle with any remaining marinade. Cover the grill and cook for 3 to 5 minutes or until the cheeses are swollen and ready to burst.
- Serve the cheeses on a platter with grilled ciabatta. To eat, make a shallow cut on top of cheese and party peel back skin. Dunk bread in melted cheese and go for it! Serve with Sunblushed tomatoes

- *Tip: If grilling isn't possible, lay cheese on a parchment-lined tray. Bake in a preheated 375?F oven for 3 to 5 minutes.
- Sunblushed Tomatoes In early morning, heat your oven to its top temperature. Remove the stems from the tomatoes and cut larger ones in half along their equator. Place cut side up in an ovenproof dish.
- Sprinkle with sea salt, thyme and oregano. Drizzle over the olive oil and put in the oven.
- Turn the oven temperature down to 165-200°F. The lower the temperature, the longer it will take but more flavorful they will be.
- Cook for 2-3 hours, until the tomatoes are soft and fragrant. Store in an airtight container in the fridge.
- Makes about 1 cup (can easily be multiplied, though)

50. Grilled Carrot And Chickpea Panzanella With Brie

Serving: Serves 4 people | Prep: 0hours45mins | Cook: 0hours30mins | Ready in:

Ingredients

- "Old Style" Dijon Mustard, Olive Oil, Ground Cumin, Red Wine Vinegar, Garlic, Salt, Pepper, Ground Hot Red Pepper Spice (optional)
- 1 tablespoon Dijon Mustard
- 1 tablespoon Olive Oil
- 1 teaspoon Ground Cumin
- 1 teaspoon Red Wine Vinegar
- 1/2 teaspoon Garlic
- 2 pinches Salt
- 2 pinches Pepper
- 2 pinches Ground Hot Red Pepper Spice
- Boule of Bread, tri-colored carrots, cherry tomatoes, red onion, Chickpeas, Brie, Salad Greens, Salt, Pepper
- 1 Boule of Bread- Classic and Crusty in nature
- 10 pieces Tri-Colored Carrots (medium sized)
- 15 pieces Cherry Tomatoes
- 1/2 Medium Sized Red Onion
- 1 cup Chickpeas skinned
- 4 ounces Brie Cubed (mild-medium)
- Salad greens to users preference
- Salt to users preference
- Pepper to users preference

Direction

- "Old Style" Dijon Mustard, Olive Oil, Ground Cumin, Red Wine Vinegar, Garlic, Salt, Pepper, Ground Hot Red Pepper Spice (optional)
- Combine all ingredients
- Whisk together until combined. Set Aside.
- Boule of Bread, tri-colored carrots, cherry tomatoes, red onion, Chickpeas, Brie, Salad Greens, Salt, Pepper
- Cut whole boule in half. Set one half aside to enjoy later.
- With the remaining half of bread cut it into medium cubes.
- Lay cubed pieces of bread on baking tray
- Turn oven to low broil and cook bread until toasted or slightly burned at edges per preference (Watch carefully!) (This step can also be done on the grill)
- Let bread cool once crisped.
- Clean carrots- cut tops and peel outside. (If using traditional grill skip the next step and cut carrots post grilling)
- Cut carrots into approximately 1" bites. (For any larger carrots cut 1" bite length-wise to make it easier to eat)
- Cut Cherry Tomatoes in half.
- Dice red onion.
- Prepare grill pan with oil. (Grill may also be used, but do not dice carrots prior to grilling and utilize grill basket for remaining items)
- Cook carrots and tomatoes on grill pan- agitate minimally and flip once grill marks appear and vegetables soften slightly.
- Cook onions on grill pan (or in grill basket)- agitate minimally flip once browning occurs.

- Combine carrots and onions in a bowl and set aside. Set tomatoes in another bowl.
- Panfry chickpeas with 3 TBSP hot vegetable oil for approximately 5 minutes or until browned. Drain and add to carrot and onion mixture.
- Once carrots, chickpeas and onions are complete mix with above dijon-cumin dressing. Then add tomatoes
- Salt and pepper to taste. (Heavier on the salt to bring out the flavors!)
- Add crisped bread cubes and gently combine (they will soak up the flavors!)
- Cut brie into small cubes and gently combine to mixture.
- Enjoy!

51. Grilled Chicken Burger With Brie

Serving: Serves 2 | Prep: | Cook: | Ready in:

Ingredients

- 2 skinless, boneless chicken breasts
- 1 bunch fresh spinach leaves
- 2 pieces light brie
- 2 tablespoons dijon mustard
- 2 teaspoons fresh chopped rosemary
- 1 pint salt and pepper
- 2 whole wheat buns

Direction

- Trim off fat and pound out to an even thickness
- Season with salt, pepper, and rosemary
- Grill 4-5 minutes per side over medium heat until no longer pink in the middle
- Grill buns if desired
- Assemble burgers with Dijon, spinach leaves, and brie

52. Guilty Pleasure Lunch

Serving: Serves 1 | Prep: | Cook: | Ready in:

Ingredients

- 2 slices of your favorite pumpkin bread
- 3-4 quarter inch thick slices of good brie cheese

Direction

- Make a sandwich out of the pumpkin bread and the brie slices. If desired, toast the bread first. Enjoy :)!

53. Honeyed Pear And Brie Toasts

Serving: Serves 2 as meal, 8 as appetizer | Prep: | Cook: | Ready in:

Ingredients

- 2 Whole wheat English muffins, or other bread of choice
- 1/4 pound Triple creme brie, room temperature
- 1 Pear, sliced thin
- 1-2 Sprigs thyme, leaves pulled off stems
- 1 teaspoon Honey

Direction

- Toast English muffins, then generously spread brie, top with a couple slices of pear, thyme leaves, and a little drizzle of honey.
- If serving as appetizer, use smaller pieces of bread or cut each piece in half.

54. Individual Apple Brie Pies Tartlets

Serving: Makes 4 small tartelettes | Prep: | Cook: | Ready in:

Ingredients

- 1 puff pastry
- 4 small apples
- 50 g walnuts and hazelnuts
- 2-3 splashes olive oil
- 2-3 sprigs thyme (leaves)
- 4 teaspoons grainy french mustard
- 1/2 brie

Direction

- Peel the apple and cut into dice. In a pan, heat some olive oil and cook the apple on medium heat for about 15 minutes. The apples should get "creamy." Remove from heat and add the nuts and thyme leaves
- Preheat oven on 350F
- Cut the brie into slices
- Roll out the puff pastry and make four rounds. Spread the rounds into four individuals pie pans. Prick the bottom with a fork, spread one teaspoon of mustard on each tartlet then add the apples and nuts mixture
- Cover with slices of brie (If you have some pastry left you can decorate the top with strips of puff pastry). Add a sprinkle of olive oil, salt and pepper
- Bake for about 25 minutes. You may have to cover the pies with aluminum foil if the tartlets start getting too brown.
- Serve with a side salad

55. LA VICTORIA Pineapple Verde Baked Brie

Serving: Serves 6 | Prep: | Cook: | Ready in:

Ingredients

- 1 sheet puff pastry, thawed
- 1 8 oz. round Brie cheese
- 1/2 cup LA VICTORIA® Pineapple Salsa Verde
- 1 apple, cored and thinly sliced
- 1 large egg, beaten
- crackers for serving

Direction

- Preheat oven to 400°F.
- Line baking sheet with silicone baking mat or parchment paper and set aside.
- Place thawed sheet puff pastry on work surface. Cut Brie in half horizontally. Place one-half Brie on sheet of puff pastry, cut side up. Spread LA VICTORIA® Pineapple Salsa Verde on cut side of Brie. Top with apple slices, arranging them in overlapping concentric circles. Place other half of Brie, cut side down, on top of apple slices.
- Brush edges of puff pastry with beaten egg and pull edges of puff pastry up to wrap Brie entirely. Turn puff pastry package over, smooth side up. Place wrapped Brie on baking sheet and refrigerate 10 minutes.
- To bake, brush pastry all over with beaten egg. Bake Brie until pastry is golden brown, about 30 minutes.
- Allow Brie to cool for 10 minutes before serving. Transfer to serving plate and serve warm with crackers.

56. La Pearisienne

Serving: Serves 4 | Prep: | Cook: | Ready in:

Ingredients

- Vinaigrette
- 1/3 cup extra virgin olive oil
- 1 tablespoon cider vinegar
- 1 tablespoon white wine vinegar
- 1 tablespoon maple syrup
- salt and pepper, to taste

- Salad
- 3 cups mache / rampon
- 3 cups arugula
- 2 pears, cored and cubed
- 1/4 cup almonds, toasted (I prefer almond slivers or slices)
- 7 ounces brie, cubed

Direction

- Whisk together vinaigrette ingredients. Set aside.
- Combine mache, arugula, pears and almonds in a salad bowl.
- Add 3/4 of the vinaigrette to the bowl, taste test. If it is too dry, add some more.
- Toss the salad with the brie and serve (preferably with warm whole wheat bread). Bon app!

57. Leek, Mushroom, And Roma Fritatta With Brie

Serving: Serves 6 | Prep: | Cook: | Ready in:

Ingredients

- Olive oil to film bottom of a skillet
- 2 leeks, sliced and washed as described here: http://www.food52.com/blog...howtocutand cleanleeks
- 12 mushrooms of your color choice, stemmed, 1/4" slice
- 2 roma tomatoes, stem end romoved, halved lengthwise, 1/4" slice
- 8 large eggs
- 4 ounces heavy cream
- 6 generous slices of Brie, trimmed of rind, 1/2" chunks
- sea or kosher salt and pepper

Direction

- Preheat oven to 375 degrees. Spray a baking casserole's sides and bottom with pan spray.
- Heat a skillet over medium-high heat. Add olive oil. When it shimmers, add leeks along with a dusting of good sea or kosher salt. Stir now and then, and as they begin to soften, add sliced mushrooms along with another good dash of salt to hasten release of their water. When their juices begin to thicken in the bottom of the skillet, add tomatoes, and as their juices begin to collect, remove from heat.
- In a mixing bowl whisk together eggs and cream. Stir in chunks of Brie, then stir in buttery soft leeks, mushrooms, and tomatoes. Add a dash of salt and some fresh ground pepper. Turn into your prepared casserole dish. Place in oven and bake for 30 minutes, rotating at the 15-minute point. Frittata is done when you can bounce a finger off the top and it feels springy with a bit of tenderness lingering. It shouldn't feel rubbery. Remove from oven, cover with your prettiest kitchen towel, and let sit for 10 minutes before serving.
- Buon apetito!

58. Maple Brie Sweet Potato Gratin

Serving: Serves 4 | Prep: | Cook: | Ready in:

Ingredients

- 1 large or 2 small sweet potatoes, not more than 1 pound total
- 4.5 ounce round of Brie au Bleu
- Soft butter for brushing the casserole
- 1 teaspoon sea or kosher salt
- Several grinds of pepper
- 2 ounces of your favorite maple syrup, medium amber
- 6 ounces heavy cream

Direction

- Preheat oven to 375 degrees.
- Peel the sweet potato (es) and slice them as thin as possible. This is an excellent job for the thin setting on a mandoline.

- Trim the rind from around the edge of the round of brie, then carefully slice off both the bottom and top rinds. There is nothing objectionable about their flavor - in fact, they're very tender and you should definitely eat them with some good bread or crackers. Rather, the cheese will melt to a much better consistency within the gratin with the rind removed. Slice the Brie thinly, narrower than 1/2".
- Run a pastry brush over some soft butter, then brush the inside of a 2-quart casserole, hopefully with a lid.
- Arrange half of the sweet potato slices in the bottom of the casserole, fanning them apart with your fingers. Try to get the layer as level as possible. Sprinkle 1/2 teaspoon of salt over them, followed by some grinds of pepper. Drizzle 1 ounce of maple syrup over the sweet potatoes, followed by 3 ounces of heavy cream. Arrange the slices of Brie in a single layer. Over the Brie, distribute the remaining slices of sweet potato. Sprinkle with another 1/2 teaspoon of salt and some grinds of pepper. Pour over them the remaining ounce of maple syrup and the last 3 ounces of cream. Cover with a lid or aluminum foil and place in oven.
- Bake for 20 minutes, then remove the lid or foil and bake for another 20 minutes. The gratin is done when the potatoes feel tender when pierced with a sharp knife, the cream is reduced and thickened, and the surface is lightly browned. Remove from oven, replace lid or foil, and let sit for 5 minutes before serving.

59. Mini Phyllo Wrapped Brie With Honey And Pistachios

Serving: Makes 12 | Prep: | Cook: | Ready in:

Ingredients

- 1 Brie wedge cut into 12 one-inch cubes
- 1 Package phyllo dough
- 1/2 cup Toasted pistachios
- 1/2 cup honey
- Melted butter for brushing

Direction

- Unwrap the phyllo dough and lay one sheet on a counter or cook surface. Brush sheet with melted butter, layer another phyllo sheet on top and brush with butter. Repeat twice to make a stack of four sheets.
- Cut the phyllo dough stack in half, width wise, and place one brie cube on each section.
- Top brie with about 1 tsp. pistachios and drizzle with honey.
- Gather the edges of the phyllo dough to create a pouch around the cheese. Slightly twist the dough at the top to secure being careful not to rip anything.
- Repeat the steps with the remaining sheets until all of the cheese is used.
- Bake according to the package watching closely so the tops do not burn.

60. Montrachet Tarts

Serving: Makes 6 cocktail servings | Prep: | Cook: | Ready in:

Ingredients

- Brie Puff Pastry
- 1 cup unsalted butter, COLD (cut into 8 pieces)
- 2 cups organic unbleached flour
- 4 ounces imported Brie cheese, at room temperature
- Making the Tarts
- 1 recipe Brie Puff Pastry
- 1 cup extra virgin olive oil
- 1-2 branches fresh rosemary
- 1 log mild goat cheese

Direction

- Brie Puff Pastry
- In the food processor fitted with the metal blade, combine the flour and butter with short pulses until mixture is the consistency of coarse meal.
- Cut the Brie into several small pieces and add to the flour mixture. Pulse until just before mixture forms a ball. Form mixture into a disc and refrigerate for at least 1/2 hour.
- Teacher's Tip: This pastry is so versatile and durable you may wish to make it in "commercial amounts" and keep it on hand in your freezer. Here are the proportions: 1 pound unsalted butter, 1 pound (4 cups) unbleached flour; 1/2 pound Brie.
- Making the Tarts
- Remove the rosemary leaves from their stems and chop them coarsely with a large chef's knife. Put into a glass jar with the olive oil. You may do this several days (weeks) ahead.
- When you are ready to assemble the tarts, pull small pieces of the dough (about the size of a gumball) from the disc, and roll into a ball in your palms. Place the balls about 1 inch apart on a baking sheet. Press them down with your thumb. Put a little piece of goat cheese in the thumbprint. Chill the trays VERY WELL.
- Preheat the oven to 425 degrees F. Remove baking sheets from refrigerator only as needed. Brush each tart with the room-temperature rosemary oil. Bake about 10 minutes. Remove to a tray and serve immediately.
- Teacher's Tip: Garnish the serving tray with a fresh rosemary sprig.

61. Mushroom Soup With Red Wine And Brie

Serving: Serves 4 | Prep: | Cook: | Ready in:

Ingredients

- 2 tablespoons butter
- 2 tablespoons olive oil
- 2 onions, sliced
- 4 cloves garlic, minced
- 6 ounces crimini mushrooms, quartered
- 4 ounces oyster mushrooms, chopped
- 1 cup red wine
- 4 cups beef stock
- 2 bay leaves
- 1 bunch thyme
- 4 ounces baguette
- 4 ounces brie
- salt and pepper

Direction

- Melt the butter and garlic in a soup pan set over medium heat. Add the onions and garlic and cook until soft and golden, about 15 minutes. Add the mushrooms and cook for another 5 minutes. Stir in the stock, wine, bay leaves, and thyme. Bring to a boil, then reduce heat and simmer for 30 minutes. Remove and discard bay leaves. Season to taste with salt and pepper.
- Spread each baguette slice with some Brie. Place two slices in the bottom of each of four bowls. Spoon the hot soup over top to melt the cheese.

62. Mushroom Soup With Wheat Berries, Kale, And Brie

Serving: Serves 4-6 | Prep: | Cook: | Ready in:

Ingredients

- 2 1\2 tablespoons unsalted butter
- 1 medium onion, diced
- 4 celery stalks, chopped
- 1 1/2 pounds mushrooms, sliced (I used crimini, but baby bellas or white button would do nicely)
- 1/2 teaspoon ground sea salt
- 1/2 teaspoon ground black pepper
- 4 garlic cloves, minced

- 1 tablespoon fresh sage leaves, minced
- 1 teaspoon dried rosemary
- 1/2 teaspoon dried red pepper flake
- 3 tablespoons all-purpose flour
- 1 cup dry white wine, such as Sauvignon Blanc or Pinot Grigio
- 6 cups vegetable broth
- 1 bay leaf
- 3/4 cup dry wheat berries (I used red wheat berries)
- 3 cups kale, de-ribbed and chopped
- 1/4 cup heavy cream
- 1/3 cup brie, rind removed and crumbled into small pieces

Direction

- In a Dutch oven or large pot, heat the butter over medium-high heat. Add the onion and celery and cook, stirring occasionally, for about 5 minutes, until onions are translucent.
- Add the mushrooms and the salt and pepper and cook, stirring occasionally, for 20-25 minutes, until the mushrooms have released their liquids and the liquids have begun to reduce.
- Add the garlic, sage, rosemary, and red pepper and cook for an additional 2 minutes.
- Add the flour and stir to incorporate, forming a roux.
- Add the wine and allow it to reduce, about 6-8 minutes.
- Slowly add the vegetable stock, and then the bay leaf, and stir, making sure to scrape the bottom of the pan.
- Add the wheat berries and stir to incorporate. Bring the soup to a boil and then reduce the heat to low and simmer, covered, for 20 minutes.
- Add the kale, cream, and brie, and continue to simmer, covered, for 10-15 minutes, until the kale is tender.
- Remove from heat and let the soup sit for 10-15 minutes, allowing the wheat berries to continue to soak up the broth. Serve with homemade croutons or crusty bread, if desired.

63. Pasta With Tomatoes, Garlic, Basil & Brie

Serving: Serves 6 as a main course | Prep: 8hours0mins | Cook: 0hours15mins | Ready in:

Ingredients

- 3/4 pound Brie (triple cream if you can get it)
- 4 medium ripe-as-can-be tomatoes
- 2 medium cloves garlic
- 1/2 cup loosely packed basil leaves, cleaned and dried
- 1/2 cup plus 2 tablespoons excellent olive oil
- 1 dash Kosher or sea salt and freshly ground pepper
- 1 pound curly pasta (I like cavatappi)

Direction

- Put the Brie in the freezer for about 20 minutes to firm up a little. This will make it easier to cut when the time comes.
- Roughly chop the tomatoes and put them in a large serving bowl. Finely chop the garlic and add it to the bowl. Chiffonade or roughly chop the basil and add that to the bowl too. Pour in the olive oil and add a generous amount of salt and pepper. Gently stir everything together.
- Once the Brie is firm enough, cut it into 1/2-inch cubes and add these to the bowl. Gently fold to combine the cheese with the rest of the ingredients. Cover the bowl and let it sit at room temperature for at least 2, and up to 8, hours -- the longer the better.
- When you are ready to eat, bring a large pot of heavily salted water to a boil and cook the pasta until just al dente. Strain it and tip it into the bowl with the sauce. Fold everything together until it is well combined, the Brie has begun to melt, and the pasta is slicked with cheese and tomato goodness. Serve immediately with a big green salad.

64. Pear Bacon And Brie Crust....eenies

Serving: Serves 6 or more | Prep: | Cook: | Ready in:

Ingredients

- 1/3 cup walnuts, toasted
- 3 slices bacon, fried crispy and crumbled
- 8 ounces brie cheese
- 1 ripe pear
- 6 ounces cream cheese, softened
- 2 loaves french bread

Direction

- Toast the walnuts by placing in a dry pan and toasting until fragrant.
- Fry bacon till crisp, drain on paper towels and crumble into a bowl.
- Remove rind from brie and dice.
- Core and dice the pear.
- Combine everything together except the bread.
- Slice the French bread into 1/4 inch slices and toast under the broiler on both sides.
- Place about a rounded tablespoon of brie walnut pear mixture on each slice of toast.

65. Pear, Ham And Brie Galette

Serving: Serves 4 | Prep: | Cook: | Ready in:

Ingredients

- 1 1/4 cups flour
- 1/4 teaspoon salt
- 1 stick of butter (8 Tbsp)
- 1 ounce water
- 1/3 cup crème fraîche (or in a pinch sub sour cream)
- 6 ounces smoked ham, thinly sliced
- 4 ounces brie cheese, sliced
- 2 small pears, sliced
- 2 teaspoons fresh thyme leaves
- 1 egg, beaten until smooth

Direction

- Measure the flour into a large bowl. Add the salt, and stir to mix it in.
- Being careful to handle the butter as little as possible (you want to keep it cold, and body heat will warm it up), cut the butter into small pieces, then add to the flour.
- Using your hands, work the butter into the flour until the pieces are small (about the size of a pea) and the mixture has a grainy texture.
- Add the water (very cold) a little bit at a time, mixing until the dough is all incorporated into a ball. If 1 oz of water doesn't seem to be enough, you can add a bit more, but add it a little bit at a time, and use the least amount of water possible to hold the dough together.
- Flatten the dough into a disc, wrap in plastic and refrigerate for at least 15-20 minutes before working with it further.
- Take dough out of the refrigerator, and on a well-floured surface, roll dough out to a circle of approximately 12 inch diameter. Transfer to the lined baking sheet.
- Spread the crème fraîche evenly in the center of the dough circle, leaving a 2-3 inch border around the edges. Top evenly with the ham and brie slices, and arrange the pears on top. Sprinkle evenly with the thyme leaves.
- Fold edges up around the filling. Brush any exposed crust with the beaten egg, then place in the oven and bake until golden brown, about 25-30 minutes. Cool before eating.

66. Persimmon Grilled Cheese W/ Goat Cheddar & Prosciutto

Serving: Serves 2 | Prep: | Cook: | Ready in:

Ingredients

- 4 slices of your favorite bread
- 2 tablespoons grainy mustard
- 1 fuyu persimmon, peeled and sliced
- 6 large slices of goat cheddar cheese (or goat brie or regular cheddar)
- 4 slices of prosciutto
- melted butter or olive oil for brushing

Direction

- Heat a skillet over a medium flame. Add the prosciutto slices and cook until just crisp on both sides. It will only take a couple of minutes. Wash the pan and return it to the stove. Heat it over medium-low heat.
- Spread the mustard on one side of all the bread. To two slices of bread add a layer of cheese, then the persimmons, another layer of cheese, then the prosciutto, and finally a third layer of cheese. Top with the remaining bread.
- Brush the tops and bottoms of the sandwiches with melted butter or olive oil and place in the preheated pan. Cook slowly, turning frequently, until the sandwiches are a deep golden brown and the cheese is melted (note: goat cheddar doesn't melt as much as goat brie or regular cheddar).
- Slice each sandwich in half and serve immediately.

67. Polenta Cakes With Caramelized Onions, Brie And Basil Oil

Serving: Makes 35-40 | Prep: | Cook: | Ready in:

Ingredients

- Polenta Cakes + Brie
- 4 cups chicken stock
- 1 cup instant polenta
- 1/2 cup half and half
- 1/2 teaspoon garlic powder
- 1 large yellow onion
- brie cheese, cut into 1-inch squares
- 2 tablespoons olive oil or butter
- salt and pepper
- Basil Oil
- 1/4 cup fresh basil
- 1/4 cup extra virgin olive oil
- 1 garlic clove
- salt and pepper

Direction

- Combine basil, extra virgin olive oil, garlic clove, salt and pepper in a food processor. Blend for about 3 minutes until all the ingredients are incorporated. Set aside.
- Bring chicken stock to a boil. Add polenta, stirring continuously for about 3 minutes. Stir in half and half, salt, pepper and garlic powder. Pour into 13x9 greased baking dish. Cover with plastic wrap and refrigerate for about 4 hours.
- Meanwhile, heat olive oil over medium heat in a large skillet. Add onions and stir occasionally for 15 minutes. As the onions begin to caramelize and turn darker, stir more frequently, about every 60 seconds, for 10 to 15 minutes. Entire process should take between 25-30 minutes. Season with salt and pepper to taste.
- To assemble, cut polenta into 1½ inch squares. Top with slice of brie cheese and about 1 teaspoon of caramelized onions. Drizzle with basil oil for garnish.

68. Pumpkin Bread With Brie

Serving: Makes 1 loaf | Prep: | Cook: | Ready in:

Ingredients

- 1 2/3 cups all purpose flour
- 1 1/2 teaspoons baking powder
- 1/2 teaspoon baking soda
- 1 tablespoon ground cinnamon
- 1 teaspoon freshly ground nutmeg

- 1/4 teaspoon ground cloves
- 1 cup 2 Tbs. pumpkin puree
- 1 cup melted coconut oil (or you can replace this with vegetable oil)
- 3/4 cup sugar
- 1/3 cup dark brown sugar
- 3/4 teaspoon salt
- 3 large eggs at room temperature
- 1 wedge of Brie - enough for everybody eating to have a couple thin slices

Direction

- Heat your oven to 350F. Grease a 9X5 loaf pan.
- In one bowl, combine the flour, baking soda, baking powder, cinnamon, nutmeg, and cloves.
- In a large bowl, beat together the pumpkin, oil, sugars, and salt until well blended. Beat in the eggs one at a time, beating until completely incorporated. Stir in the dry ingredients just until blended.
- Scrape the batter into the prepared loaf pan and bake until a toothpick stuck into the bread comes out clean, about an hour.
- Allow the bread to cool in the pan for about 20 minutes before removing it. Serve thick warm slices topped with pieces of the Brie. You can also toast leftovers and serve with Brie.

69. Red Onion & Apple Gastrique Tartlets

Serving: Makes 12 | Prep: | Cook: | Ready in:

Ingredients

- Dough
- 1 egg yolk
- 2 tablespoons ice water
- 1 teaspoon vanilla extract
- 1 1/4 cups AP flour
- 1/3 cup sugar
- 1/4 teaspoon salt
- 8 tablespoons cold, unsalted butter (1 stick)
- Filling
- 2 red apples (peeled & sliced thin) (pink lady is a good choice)
- 2 red onions (sliced thin)
- 1/2 cup dark brown sugar
- 1/4 cup water
- 1/2 cup apple cider vinegar
- 1 cup apple cider
- pinch salt
- 3/4 cup brie

Direction

- We're gonna do the dough first. Mix together the flour, sugar, and salt in a big bowl.
- Cut the stick of butter into roughly ¼" cubes and mix it in with a pastry cutter. You want to end up with pieces the size of small pebbles, so don't mix it up too much.
- Whisk together the egg yolk, water, and vanilla, and add it all to the butter/flour mixture with a fork. If it starts to give you a little resistance and clump up, you're good.
- Put some flour on a big cutting board or other flat thing, and dump the dough on top of it.
- Roll the dough into a ball, then flatten it into a disk. Wrap it in plastic wrap and put it in the fridge for 30 minutes.
- Preheat your oven to 400.
- Put more flour on your cutting board and more flour on a rolling pin. Just throw the whole damn bag of flour at your kitchen Rip Taylor-style; you're gonna want a lot of it.
- Roll the dough to about ¼" thick, then cut it into rounds and press it into whatever fancy-ass tiny tart molds you got. And make sure to spray them with non-stick if they're metal.
- Put the little tartlets on a baking sheet and bake for about 15 minutes, until they start to get a little golden brown and toasty. Let them rest on a baking sheet for 5 minutes after they come out. You know the drill.
- Now's a good time to start on the filling.
- Mix together the brown sugar and water in a big, wide pan over low heat. Let them get comfortable for a while, until they're

simmering and starting to caramelize and turn a little darker.
- Slowly add in the vinegar, followed by the cider, and let them simmer and reduce for a bit, about 10 minutes.
- You're gonna do two different things here: get a smaller pan and pour a little of the gastrique you just made (yes, that's what it's called) in, just enough to cover the bottom.
- Put the onions and a pinch of salt in, stir, and let them caramelize while you keep stirring. It should take about 15 minutes.
- At the same time, put the apples in the bigger pot (remember, that's gonna be full of most of the gastrique) and poach 'em for about 5 minutes, until they're limp but not mushy or falling apart. Basically, just keep an eye on them and make sure they don't start turning gross.
- Once the tartlets, mini-tarts, tartinis, whatever-the-hell-you-want-to-call-ems are cool, put some of the onions in each and layer the sliced apples on top, followed by about a tablespoon of brie per tart.
- Set your oven to 350 and put the tarts in again, just until the brie melts. Shouldn't take more than a minute or two.
- Eat.

70. Roast Turkey, Brie, Cranberry Sandwich On Walnut Bread

Serving: Serves one sandwich | Prep: | Cook: |Ready in:

Ingredients

- 3/4 cup roast turkey, roughly shredded
- 3 or 4 slices of triple creme Brie
- 2 tablespoons cranberry sauce, preferably homemade
- 1/4 cup baby arugula or spinach
- 2 thick slices of walnut bread
- Extra virgin olive oil
- Fresh ground pepper

Direction

- Lightly brush both sides of bread with olive oil.
- Place arugula on one slice of bread, top with turkey, brie and cranberry sauce. Add a little fresh ground pepper. Place the other piece of bread on top.
- Cook in a panini press for 3-4 minutes or in a non-stick frying pan pressing down with a spatula or heavy pan. (If using a frying pan, you will need to flip the sandwich after 2 minutes.)
- Cut the sandwich in half and serve with a glass of Pinot Noir.

71. Roasted Garlic Baked Brie

Serving: Serves 8 | Prep: | Cook: |Ready in:

Ingredients

- 1 whole garlic bulb
- 2 1/2 teaspoons olive oil
- 1 round loaf sourdough bread
- 1 round (8 oz) brie cheese
- 1 loaf french baguette sliced
- 1 Tablespoon fresh rosemary (or 1 tsp dried rosemary) OPTIONAL
- assorted apples, grapes, pears, crackers for serving

Direction

- Preheat oven to 425°.
- Cut off the top of the garlic bulb to reveal a portion of the cloves. Drizzle with 1.5 teaspoons oil and sprinkle with rosemary (if using). Wrap it up in foil and bake at 425° for 30-35 minutes, until softened. Set aside to cool (10-15 minutes). Reduce heat to 375°.
- When the garlic is cooling, cut off the top fourth of the loaf of bread and carefully hollow it out so that the brie can sit inside. Set

aside the removed bread and place the brie cheese inside the bread.
- Once cooled, gently squeeze the softened garlic cloves into a small bowl and mash with a fork. Spread the garlic mixture over the brie cheese and replace the bread top. Brush the outside of the bread with a teaspoon of oil and wrap in foil, sealing the edges.
- Bake the bread for 45-50 minutes or until cheese is melted. Serve with toasted baguette, apples, grapes, crackers and reserved bread cubes.

- Preheat broiler. Spread half of the cheese mixture on 12 halves toasts. Season with pepper. Broil until cheese bubbles (watch it carefully to make sure they don't burn). Sprinkle with parsley. Transfer to a platter.
- Stir in the avocados, zest and juice of 1 lime into remaining half of the cheese mixture, taste and add salt (if needed); spread this mixture on the remaining muffin halves. Do not broil these toasts; just season with pepper, sprinkle with cilantro, transfer to the same platter and serve.

72. Roasted Garlic And Brie Toasts

Serving: Serves makes 12 | Prep: | Cook: | Ready in:

Ingredients

- • 12 English Muffins, separated
- • 1 ½ tablespoons olive oil
- • 1 large garlic head, cloves separated (unpeeled)
- • 12 ounces ripe Brie cheese, rind removed, room temperature
- •   A generous pinch of cayenne pepper
- • Chopped fresh parsley and cilantro
- • 2 ripe Hass avocados
- • Zest and juice of 1 lime

Direction

- Preheat oven to 350 degrees Fahrenheit. Place 12 muffin halves on a cookie sheet. Bake until golden (about 10 minutes). Cool. Heat olive oil in a heavy small ovenproof skillet over medium heat. Add garlic and toss to coat.
- Transfer skillet to oven and bake garlic until knife pierces centers easily (about 20 minutes). Cool slightly. Peel garlic. Transfer garlic to bowl and mash with fork. Add Brie and cayenne pepper and mix well. (You can make it 6 hours ahead, just cover and let it stand at room temperature.)

73. Roasted Garlic, Avocado, Brie And Green Sauce Dip

Serving: Serves a crowd | Prep: | Cook: | Ready in:

Ingredients

- For the roasted garlic, avocado and brie base
- • 1 ½ tablespoons avocado extra-virgin or pure olive oil
- • 1 medium head garlic cloves, separated (unpeeled)
- • 8 ounces ripe Brie cheese, rind removed, room temperature
- • 2 ripe Hass avocados, pitted and peeled
- • 1/4 teaspoon cayenne pepper
- • Zest and juice of 1medium lime
- For the green sauce
- • 3/4 cup packed cilantro leaves
- • 3/4 cup packed basil leaves
- • 1/2 cup green raw pistachios or pepitas, toasted
- • 5 tablespoons extra-virgin avocado or olive oil
- • 1 1/2 teaspoons red-wine vinegar
- • Salt and freshly ground pepper to taste

Direction

- Preheat oven to 350 degrees F. Heat oil in a heavy small ovenproof skillet over medium heat. Add garlic and toss to coat. Transfer

skillet to oven and bake garlic until knife pierces centers easily (about 20 minutes). Cool slightly and peel. Toast pistachios until slightly browned and fragrant; cool.
- Transfer garlic to a bowl and mash with fork; add Brie, avocado, lime juice and zest and cayenne pepper; stir until smooth and well combined.
- Place cilantro, basil and pistachios in a food processor; add oil, vinegar, salt and pepper to taste; puree and then using a rubber spatula, fold into the garlic, Brie and avocado mixture, leaving a trace of the green sauce. Serve chilled or at room temperature.

74. Roasted Garlic, Onion & Chicken Soup

Serving: Serves 2 | Prep: | Cook: | Ready in:

Ingredients

- Garlic-Onion-Chicken Broth
- 1 whole head of garlic
- 4 tablespoons olive oil, divided
- 4 cloves of raw garlic, peeled and thinly sliced
- 2 onions, peeled and roughly chopped
- 1 whole chicken carcass, with chicken reserved, some skin removed, and carcass cut into pieces
- 1 cup red wine
- 3 tablespoons fresh thyme, stems roughly chopped
- 10 cups water
- 1 teaspoon salt
- 1/2 teaspoon freshly ground black pepper
- Roasted Garlic, Onion & Chicken Soup
- 4 cups garlic-onion-chicken broth
- 1 cup shredded chicken
- 1/2 cup tiny elbow pasta
- 2 tablespoons finely chopped chives
- salt and pepper, to taste
- 2 4-inch pieces of fresh baguette, sliced in half
- 4 thick slices of room temperature Brie

Direction

- Make the smashed roasted garlic: Set your oven to 350 degrees. Slice the entire top quarter of the head of garlic off, exposing all the fresh garlic. Set the garlic in a small casserole and drizzle 2 tablespoons of olive oil on top. Roast in the oven for 45-60 minutes until the garlic is soft and golden brown. Remove from the oven and cool until easy to handle. Squeeze the garlic cloves from the garlic skin shell. With the back of a spoon, mash the cloves until a thick paste is formed. Set aside.
- In heavy bottom pan over medium-high heat, warm the olive oil until hot. Toss in the onions and raw garlic cloves, permitting 5 minutes for the vegetables to soften and get a little golden in color. Add the chicken carcass pieces, allowing them to also caramelize slightly as well.
- Slowly, as it will sizzle, pour in the red wine and sprinkle in the fresh thyme. Let the wine return to a simmer to burn off some alcohol, and occasionally scrape the bottom of the pan to pick up some of the brown bits.
- Add in the water and bring to a boil. Then cover and simmer on medium-low heat for 90 minutes, adding a little water in here or there to maintain about 90% of the volume.
- At the 90-minute mark, stir in the smashed roasted garlic, salt and pepper. Let flavors meld and simmer an additional 30 minutes.
- Strain the broth and retain only the liquid. Store the broth in the fridge for 2-3 days or freeze or use immediately.
- Roasted Garlic, Onion & Chicken Soup
- Warm the broth over medium heat in a soup pot. Add the chicken, pasta, and chives and simmer for 10 minutes. Add salt and pepper, to taste. Divide the soup between two bowls.
- Serve with baguette and brie, divided evenly.
- Note: As a delicious alternative, boil the broth and crack the contents of a farm fresh egg into the boiling liquid. After 3-4 minutes, when the

egg whites have become opaque and solid, pour the soup and egg into a bowl. Break the yolk with your spoon and enjoy.

75. Roasted Pineapple Heirloom Tomato And Brie Bruschetta

Serving: Makes 10 pieces | Prep: | Cook: | Ready in:

Ingredients

- 2 large pineapple heirloom tomatoes, sliced 1/4 inch thick
- 2 tablespoons olive oil
- 1 pinch fine sea salt
- 1 pinch cracked pepper
- 2 teaspoons dried basil
- 10 slices sour dough baguette, cut 1/2 inch thick
- 2 cloves garlic, peeled
- 10 slices brie, cut 1/4 inch thick

Direction

- Preheat oven to 375 degrees F.
- Place tomato slices on a lined and greased baking sheet.
- Drizzle with olive oil and sprinkle with salt, pepper and dried basil.
- Roast until bubbly about 10 to 12 minutes.
- In the meantime also toast slices of baguette just until golden but still slightly chewy.
- Rub partially toasted baguette with clove of garlic, top with a slice of both the brie and tomato.
- Return to oven to finish toasting and melt cheese, about another 5 minutes.

76. Roasted Beet And Brie Sandwich

Serving: Serves 1 | Prep: | Cook: | Ready in:

Ingredients

- hard roll, or sandwich-sized section of baguette
- 1 small beet, roasted
- 1 ounce brie
- 1 handful toasted chopped walnuts
- a few sprigs fresh basil
- 1 leaf lettuce
- red wine vinegar, to taste
- salt and pepper, to taste

Direction

- Set broiler on high. Cut roll in half and beets and brie into thin slices. Top each half of roll with beets and brie, and broil until cheese is melted and brown in spots. Remove from oven and top one side with walnuts, lettuce, and basil, and the other with vinegar, salt and pepper. Place halves together and enjoy!

77. Sauteed Brie And Shrimp

Serving: Serves 6-8 | Prep: | Cook: | Ready in:

Ingredients

- 1 pound Peeled, deveined, raw shrimp, 26-30 count or larger, seasoned with salt and pepper.
- 2-3 tablespoons Butter, divided
- 2 Cloves Garlic, minced
- 1 1/2 tablespoons Lemon juice, from about 1/2 small lemon
- 2 tablespoons Brandy
- 1- 13 ounces Wheel of Brie, Rind trimmed around edges only
- 1/3 cup Sliced almonds
- 1 tablespoon Parsley, minced
- 1 French bagette, sliced

Direction

- Preheat a 10" skillet over med-high heat. Melt half of the butter.

- Add shrimp and sauté until just pink about 1 minute each side, adding garlic half way through cooking.
- Add lemon juice and brandy. Shake pan to mix. Transfer shrimp and juices to a bowl.
- Add remaining butter to pan, then add brie wheel. Scatter almonds around brie. Let brie brown on one side, 1-2 mins. Covering pan will encourage melting.
- Flip brie over, stir almonds and let brie brown on other side, covering until melted, 1-2 minutes more.
- Add shrimp back to pan, Sprinkle with parsley. Allow shrimp to warm up 30 seconds, then plate up.
- Serve with baguette slices.

78. Savory Asian Pear, Onion And Fennel Galette

Serving: Serves 6-8 | Prep: | Cook: | Ready in:

Ingredients

- Dough
- 1/2 pound cold unsalted butter, cut into 1/2" pieces
- 2 cups all-purpose flour
- 1 teaspoon kosher salt
- 1/4 cup ice water
- Pear, Onion and Fennel Filling
- 2 medium yellow onions, peeled and thinly sliced cross-wise
- 1 small/medium fennel bulb, outer layer removed, and white/light green parts thinly sliced crosswise (discard dark green parts)
- 3 large, ripe but firm Asian pears (I used Shinko variety), peeled, cored and cut into thin slices
- 1 tablespoon unsalted butter
- 2 tablespoons extra virgin olive oil
- 1/2 teaspoon kosher salt
- 1/4 cup dry sherry
- 1 tablespoon finely chopped fresh rosemary
- 6 ounces Brie (a mild, double-cream works best)
- 1 cup grated Manchego cheese
- 1 egg
- 1 tablespoon water
- Salt and freshly ground pepper

Direction

- Dough
- Put the flour and salt in a food processor and pulse a few times to combine.
- Add the butter, tossing quickly to coat each piece with flour to prevent pieces from sticking together. Pulse until combined, and mixture is the texture of course sand.
- Add the ice water with the motor running. Process until dough comes together, stopping before it becomes a solid mass.
- Turn contents onto a clean work surface and press together with your hands, forming a ball, and then flatten into a rough disk.
- Cover dough in plastic wrap and refrigerate for at least an hour, or up to 2 days.
- Pear, Onion and Fennel Filling
- Heat butter and olive oil in a large sauté pan over medium-high heat.
- Add onions and fennel to pan and sauté until soft and translucent, stirring occasionally, about 15-20 min. Add 1/2 tsp. kosher salt.
- When liquid from onions has evaporated and mixture is beginning to brown around edges and stick to bottom of pan, add sherry to deglaze the pan, scraping the brown bits from the bottom of the pan with a wooden spoon.
- Reduce heat to low and add pears and rosemary, tossing with wooden spoon to combine. Cook for 1-2 minutes until flavors combine and pears begin to soften slightly. Add ground pepper and more salt to taste. Remove pan from heat and set aside.
- Preheat oven to 450 degrees.
- Roll out the dough on a lightly floured surface with a rolling pin into a free-form circle, about 10-12" in diameter. Transfer the dough to the center of a baking sheet.

- Remove the rind from Brie, and spread it in an even layer onto the dough leaving a 1 1/2 inch border on the outside. Spread pear and onion mixture over brie, and top with grated Manchego.
- Fold the border over the filling, gently pinching to form soft pleats every inch or so all the way around. Shape should be rustic and free-form.
- Make an egg wash by whisking egg and water together in a small bowl. Use a pastry brush to lightly coat the dough of the tart with egg wash.
- Bake the tart in the center of the oven for about 25 minutes, until the crust is golden, and the filling is bubbling with and browned on top. Cool slightly and serve warm or at room temperature.

79. Savory Crescents With Brie, Apples And Date Berry Sauce

Serving: Serves 4 | Prep: | Cook: | Ready in:

Ingredients

- 30 pieces Dates, pitted and chopped small
- 12 ounces Whole cranberries (1 bag)
- 1/2 cup Brewed black, chai, or pumpkin spiced tea
- 1 Cinnamon stick
- 2 Star Anise
- 1 tablespoon Vanilla extract
- 1 Tube Crescent rolls of choice
- 8 Slices Brie
- 1/4 cup Blueberries
- 1 Granny Smith apple, sliced thin

Direction

- Bring the cranberries, dates, vanilla, tea and spices to a boil, then simmer until the cranberries have burst and the dates are softened, and the mixture thickens slightly.
- Remove the cinnamon and star anise, and cool. Then, pulse the mixture in a food processor.
- Next, line a sheet pan with parchment, pop the crescent roll tube and lay out the pieces onto the sheet pan.
- Lay one to two slices of apple on each crescent, depending on the thickness. Divide the Brie and blueberries among the 8 crescent pieces.
- Place 2 tablespoons of the date-cranberry mixture into each crescent, then roll each crescent. I usually roast the rest of the apple slices for a snack, they usually fit on the same sheet pan.
- Bake at 350 degrees for about 10 minutes, rotate once and watch carefully as you might need to add or decrease the time to melt the Brie and get a golden color on the rolls. Enjoy!

80. Smoked Apple & Brie Cheese Cake

Serving: Serves 8 | Prep: | Cook: | Ready in:

Ingredients

- Cheese Cake
- 750g Cream Cheese
- 1.5 tablespoons Cornstarch
- 244g Sugar
- 4 Eggs
- 2 Thinly Sliced Granny Smith Apples
- fried Brie Package
- 150g Brie Cheese
- 1 Egg
- 1/4 cup Milk
- 1/2 cup Flour
- 100g Sliced Almonds
- Florentine Cheese Cake Base
- 55g Butter
- 150g Sugar
- 45g Honey
- 45g Cream
- 180g Almonds
- 60g Chopped Walnuts

- 60g Bread Flour
- balsamic   Reduction
- 500 milliliters Balsamic Vinegar
- 1 Diced Granny Smith Apple
- 150g Sugar
- 1 log Applewood
- 5 Cinnamon Sticks
- 4 Whole Cloves
- 500 milliliters Cheapest Cooking Sherry you can buy

Direction

- Let's start with the apple balsamic reduction, take the balsamic vinegar, sugar, and diced apples and bring to a boil in a sauce pan or skillet (the shallower the vessel the faster it will reduce). Once the mixture has reached a boil reduce the heat to get a light boil. Let mixture reduce for 10 to 15 minutes until the mixture is thick and bubbles become small and very close together.
- While the balsamic mixture is reducing start on the Florentine bottom for the cheese cake start by greasing a spring form pan and set aside. Bring the butter and sugar to a boil in a small sauce pan. Whisk the egg and temper it into your butter mixture. Add the toasted nuts and flour to the egg and butter mixture and stir together poor this into the spring form pan and bake for 10 to 15 minutes or until the Florentine is a light golden brown.
- Ok now I will explain how to smoke the cheese cake, I used my brick wood fired oven, but you can use a BBQ as well. Take apple wood chips or if you are using a brick oven you can use a small log, soak it in cheap sherry or another type of flammable liquor and place it on a tin baking sheet along with the cinnamon and cloves at the bottom of your BBQ (you may have to remove some of the charcoal to make room). Light the wood on fire and turn the BBQ to high, as soon as you see smoke coming from the BBQ turn it to low.
- The cheese cake is a very simple recipe, cream the cream cheese by itself until it is smooth and free of lumps, mix the sugar and cornstarch together and mix with the cream cheese, once incorporated add the eggs one at a time fallowed by the vanilla extract and mix until fully incorporated. Poor the cheese cake batter into the pan with the florentine base and layer the apples on top going around the outside of the pan and working your way inward. Place the cheese cake in the BBQ and bake for 20-25 minutes or until the cake sets up; it should jiggle a little like jello but not slosh. The cheese cake may be a little black on top but it is not burnt it is the smoke. Allow the cheese cake to sit at room temp before transferring it to the fridge. Let it cool in the fridge for a couple hours before you try and cut it. When it comes to cutting the cheese cake use a knife submerged in hot water and after each cut wipe the blade with a cloth.
- Cut the brie into 1 cm cubes and roll it in flour, followed by egg wash, and then sliced almonds. Heat a skillet so that it is sizzling hot place a tablespoon of butter in the pan and proceed to fry the brie on all 6 sides.
- For the plating brush the balsamic reduction onto the plate and place the cheese cake perpendicular to the balsamic reduction. Place the fried brie on top of the cake and drizzle more balsamic reduction over the top of the cake and serve with some chopped granny smith apples.

81. Smoked Jalapeño Poppers With Bacon, Apple, And Brie

Serving: Makes 28 poppers | Prep: 0hours5mins | Cook: 0hours5mins |Ready in:

Ingredients

- 1/2 bacon

Direction

- Wash and dry jalapeños, cut in half, and scoop out the seeds and vein from the inside with a spoon or butter knife. Take small slices of the Brie cheese and mold into the pepper halves, then wrap one bacon piece around each pepper. Place the prepared poppers in an aluminum foil pan and set aside.

- Prepare the smoker using a fruit wood (apple, cherry, etc.). Once the smoker's temperature reaches 225F/107C degrees, place the popper's foil pan on the grill rack. Smoke for 2 hours.
- Arrange apple slices on a serving platter and place one smoked jalapeño popper on top of each slice. Serve immediately and enjoy!
- Recipe Notes & Tips:
- To bake in the oven: place the poppers on a baking sheet and bake in a preheated 400F/204C degrees for 20-30 minutes.

82. Steak Sandwich With Peach "jam" And Brie

Serving: Makes 4 sandwiches | Prep: | Cook: | Ready in:

Ingredients

- Peach Jam
- 3 large peaches, halved, cored, then sliced
- 1 medium-sized shallot, sliced
- 2 teaspoons balsamic vinegar
- 1 teaspoon honey
- 1 teaspoon granulated sugar
- 0.5 teaspoons salt
- Steak sandwich
- 2 1-pound NY Strip steaks
- 1 wedge of brie, half-pound max, at room temperature
- 8 slices of country bread
- salt and pepper to taste
- 1 tablespoon olive oil, plus more for drizzling

Direction

- For the peach jam: Preheat oven to 350 degrees. In a large bowl, combine all ingredients. Place in an 8x8 baking dish, and bake for 30 minutes. Once done, stir again to combine, then place in refrigerator to cool.
- Season steak liberally with salt and pepper. Heat a cast iron pan on medium-high and pour olive oil in to coat the pan. Cook steak, turning occasionally, until desired doneness (will depend on how you want steak cooked). Let rest for 5 minutes, then thinly slice.
- Preheat oven to 350. Line baking sheet with aluminum foil. Place slices of bread on sheet and drizzle with olive oil. Bake for 5-10 minutes or until bread is lightly toasted.
- Optional: You can place brie in the oven at this time if you'd like your brie a little hotter and easier to spread. Bake this 5-6 minutes, or until gooey but not runny.
- Layer the sandwich. Spread peach jam on one side slice of bread and brie on the other. Add steak, and season with salt and pepper.

83. Summer Tomato Linguine With Brie And Basil

Serving: Makes a huge bowl full of delicious! | Prep: | Cook: | Ready in:

Ingredients

- 4-5 pounds Fresh Tomatoes - I use the best heirlooms at the height of the summer
- 1 Wheel or Big Slice of Good Quality Brie
- 2-4 Cloves of Garlic - Crushed or Well-Chopped
- 1 bunch Fresh Basil
- Salt, Fresh Ground Pepper & Red Pepper Flakes to Taste
- 1 cup Fresh Grated Parmesan Reggiano
- Splash Fresh Lemon Juice
- 1 pound Good-Quality Linguine or Other Long, Flat Pasta Noodle
- 1/2 - 3/4 cups Extra Virgin Olive Oil - The Good One!

Direction

- Chop tomatoes into 1/2 inch dice. Add to large bowl.
- Crush or mince garlic. Add to small, microwavable bowl and top with olive oil. Microwave for about 1 to 1.5 minutes. Carefully, pour garlic and oil over tomatoes.
- Rough-chop fresh basil. Add to bowl of tomatoes and garlic.
- Cut rind completely off of the brie (it helps to keep it very cold before doing this). Dice the 'meat' of the brie and add to the bowl over the tomatoes, separating any large chunks of brie.
- Add 1/2C to 3/4C olive oil to the tomato mixture. You can always add more later, depending on how juicy the tomatoes are.
- Add about 1-2t salt to the tomato mixture, to taste, with fresh ground black pepper and red pepper flakes, to taste.
- Mix all together, cover with plastic wrap, and let marinate on the counter for as long as possible - doing it in the morning & serving it for dinner is best!
- Just before serving (if you want it hot - or anytime if you're serving it room-temperature), boil a large pot full of water and cook pasta according to the package instructions.
- When the pasta is cooked, drain and add to the large bowl of the marinated tomato mixture. Mix well. Add 1/2C grated Parmesan & a squeeze of fresh lemon juice. Mix well. Taste for salt & pepper. Add lemon, salt, pepper and red pepper flakes as needed.
- Top with more fresh chopped basil and Parmesan. Serve hot or at room temperature as a side dish or main dish with some fresh French bread or crostini! Enjoy!

84. Sweet & Savory "Vesper" Bread

Serving: Serves 1 | Prep: | Cook: |Ready in:

Ingredients

- 1 slice of your favorite bread
- unsalted, high butterfat butter
- your favorite honey
- Brie or Camembert, white rind removed
- 2 slices ham

Direction

- Warm, but do not toast your slice of bread.
- Slather it with a little butter, and then top with a little honey.
- Smear the brie cheese on top and cover with some sliced ham.
- Enjoy the melting of flavors in your mouth. (You can slice it in half and fold it over like a sandwich if it's easier to eat than open-faced)

85. Sweetbreads Crostini With On Hand Chimichurri

Serving: Serves 6-10 | Prep: | Cook: |Ready in:

Ingredients

- Chimichurri
- 1 cup Parsley
- 1 cup Cilantro
- 1 cup basil/oregano mix (or whatever floats your boat)
- 1/4 cup extra virgin olive oil
- 1/4 cup white wine vinegar
- 1 pinch ground cayenne pepper
- salt and pepper to taste
- 1 clove garlic, smashed
- Veal Sweetbreads
- 1 pound large veal sweetbreads, roughly 3
- 1 lemon
- 1/2 cup flour
- 1 cup heavy cream (optional)
- 1 baguette or quality bread, sliced and lightly toasted
- salt and pepper to taste.
- 4 tablespoons butter
- 1/4 pound fresh goat cheese or brie.

Direction

- Put the sweetbreads in a ziplock bag with ice and cold water. Let sit overnight.
- Take the sweetbreads out, put into a high-rimmed pan. Cover with water, and add the juice of the 1 lemon.
- Bring the water to a boil, turn the heat down to a simmer, cover, and let it go for 5 minutes
- Remove from heat and let the sweetbreads sit in the covered pan for another 45 minutes.
- Turn out the pan into a colander and let some cold water run over the sweetbreads. When cooled, using your best paring knife cut the sweetbreads in half lengthwise (or thick-wise)--roughly a third of an inch; trim of any tough membrane you see and then cut into four crostini-sized pieces per half.
- Put the pieces on a towel-topped plate, put a heavy cast iron skillet and top and weigh it down with whatever is heavy in your pantry. Fridge it and let sit overnight (again).
- Make the chimichurri: put all of the ingredients in a food processor and pulse it into a paste. This is about your taste; if you want it thicker, add herbs (can't over-herb it); if you like thinner, you can add a splash or oil or (if you would like tangier and thinner) vinegar.
- Optional step**: remove the sweetbreads from the weight, put in a zip-lock bag with heavy cream for 1-2 hours.
- Heat a skillet to medium-high heat (I go 8/10 on my electric stovetop but I believe my stovetop is cooler than most). Meanwhile toast your bread (can be done in advance) and bring the sweetbreads & cheese to close to room temp. I brought out the cheese and veal sb's about a half hour before cooking.
- Dredge the sweetbreads in the flour (which you should season liberally with salt) so that it is completely covered; but shake and knock off excess (it'll just burn in the fat).
- Add the butter to the pan. When hot, add the sweetbreads and fry on each side about 2 minutes per (4-5 total) until both sides get good color. The goldening butter in the pan should make your house smell like heaven. Cooking these, by the way, isn't like a burger or steak where you have to go one flip and one flip only; if you flip after 2 minutes and the color ain't there, just flip it back over. No one'll know and I won't tell...
- Assembly: either shmear some goat cheese on each piece of bread or give them a thin slice of the brie. As soon as the sweetbreads come out of the pan, place the pieces onto a respective bread/cheese piece. Spoon a bit of the chimichurri onto the top of each and serve immediately.

86. TB Cubed

Serving: Serves 1 | Prep: | Cook: |Ready in:

Ingredients

- 2 slices thick sourdough bread
- 3 slices bacon, cooked
- 2 ounces brie
- 1 roma tomato, thinly sliced
- 6 large basil leaves

Direction

- Assemble sandwich in this order (bottom to top): bread, brie, bacon, tomato, basil, bread.
- For variations, use a sourdough roll (and add more bacon and tomatoes to make a more substantial sandwich), try a different soft cheese (e.g., boursin), or (as I've done at home) get some gourmet bacon (e.g., cajun-spiced).

87. TURKEY + BRIE + AVOCADO BURGER

Serving: Serves 4 | Prep: | Cook: |Ready in:

Ingredients

- 500 grams lean ground turkey
- 1 egg

- 2 tablespoons barbecue sauce [i use sweet baby rays on everything]
- 1/2 cup panko breadcrumbs
- 1 tablespoon freshly chopped cilantro
- Pinch salt & pepper
- 1 ripe avocado
- 8 slices of brie
- 4 burger buns

Direction

- Add ground turkey, egg, barbecue sauce, breadcrumbs, cilantro, salt and pepper in a mixing bowl. Using your hands, mix all ingredients until evenly combined.
- Form meat mixture into 4 patties and refrigerate for an hour [helps firm the patties].
- Sear the burger on each side and brush with barbecue sauce.
- When the burger is cooked throughout, top with brie until it begins to melt.
- Remove from heat and top with avocado, tomato and additional barbecue sauce if you love it as much as I do.

88. Tawny Port Two Cheese Spread

Serving: Makes 1 cup | Prep: | Cook: | Ready in:

Ingredients

- 4 ounces brie
- 3 ounces crumbled gorgonzola
- 1-3 teaspoons honey
- 2 tablespoons tawny port
- 1/2 - 3/4 teaspoons quatres epices (French four spice blend)
- fine sea salt to taste

Direction

- Remove rind from brie, it's okay if small pieces remain. Cut brie into 1/4 - 3/8 inch cubes. Place brie and gorgonzola in small mixing bowl and allow to come to room temperature, about 30 minutes.
- Add remaining ingredients, starting with 1 teaspoon honey and 1/2 teaspoon quatres epices. Using hand mixer blend well. The mixture should be pretty creamy, but still have some texture. Taste and add more honey, spice, and salt if desired.
- Transfer into serving bowl. Store covered and refrigerated. Remove from refrigerator an hour before serving. Serve with good quality crackers or sliced fruit, like fuyu persimmons, acidulated pears or apples or Asian pears.

89. The Pink Poodle Pizza

Serving: Makes 1 pizza | Prep: | Cook: | Ready in:

Ingredients

- 1 12-inch pizza crust
- 4 ounces brie, cut into 10-12 thin slices, with or without the rind
- 6 slices (about 2 ounces) thinly sliced dry ham, such as jambon de pays or prosciutto
- 3 ounces chèvre
- 12 seedless red grapes, washed, dried, and halved (pole-to-pole or along the equator, your pick)
- 1/4 teaspoon dried herbes de Provence
- sea salt
- extra virgin olive oil

Direction

- Preheat oven to 425°F.
- Set pizza crust on baking tray or pizza stone.
- Lay down the strips of brie on the crust. Next, add the ham. Dot the pizza with small dollops of the chèvre and grapes. Sprinkle the entire pizza with the herbes de Provence and a little bit of salt. Drizzle a tablespoon or two of olive oil over the whole pizza.
- Bake for 10-15 minutes or until the edges of the crust just begin to brown.

- Cut and serve.
- Say "Oooh la la!" every time you take a bite.

90. Tomato & Brie Pasta

Serving: Serves 6-8 | Prep: | Cook: | Ready in:

Ingredients

- 4-6 Ripe Tomatoes, cut into small cubes
- 1/2 cup Olive oil
- 1 cup Basil Leaves
- 1 teaspoon Salt
- 1 teaspoon Pepper
- 4 Garlic Cloves, minced
- 1 Large chunk Brie cheese (3/4-1lb)
- 1 pound Cavatelli, small penne or other small pasta shape
- Salt for cooking pasta

Direction

- At least 4 hours before serving: Combine, tomatoes, S&P, olive oil and garlic in a very large bowl. Cut off the rind of the Brie, if there's some left don't worry about it. Cut into small cubes and add to tomato mixture. Cut the dry basil leaves (chiffonade) into thin strips and add. Let the ingredients marry and marinate for at least 4 hours.
- Cook pasta according to directions. Drain and pour over tomato mixture. Allow the hot pasta to wilt and "cook" the fresh ingredients. You are now ready to serve! (Top with Parmesan if desired)

91. Tomato And Basil Pasta With Brie

Serving: Serves 4 | Prep: | Cook: | Ready in:

Ingredients

- 3/4 pound Cherry tomatoes, cut into halves (or quarters if they're on the larger side)
- 1 cup Basil leaves (loose packed), roughly chopped
- 2 tablespoons Olive oil
- 1 Garlic clove, minced
- 1 teaspoon Balsamic vinegar
- 1/2 teaspoon Crushed red pepper flakes (or more to taste)
- 1/2 teaspoon Salt
- 1/2 teaspoon Pepper
- 8 ounces Brie
- 1/2 pound Pasta (I used casarecce, but linguini or fettuccine would also work great here)
- parmesan cheese for serving

Direction

- Combine the tomatoes, basil, olive oil, garlic, balsamic vinegar, red pepper flakes, salt, and pepper in a bowl.
- Cut the rind off of the brie and tear it into small pieces. Add these to the bowl with the tomato mixture. Stir to combine well, and let marinate while you cook your pasta.
- Cut the rind off of the brie and tear it into small pieces. Add these to the bowl with the tomato mixture. Stir to combine well, and let marinate while you cook your pasta.
- Season to taste with additional salt and pepper if needed, then serve immediately, topped with a sprinkle of freshly grated parmesan.

92. Tomato And Brie Tart

Serving: Serves 6-8 | Prep: | Cook: | Ready in:

Ingredients

- 2 large ripe tomatoes
- Salt to taste
- 1 sheet frozen puff pastry (from a 17-oz package)

- 1-2 tablespoons Dijon mustard or whole-grain mustard, as needed
- 1 teaspoon fresh thyme leaves
- Freshly ground black pepper to taste
- 4 ounces Brie cheese, kept cold

Direction

- Trim off the ends of the tomatoes, and slice them about 1/8 inch thick. Sprinkle the slices lightly on both sides with salt, and lay out flat between two layers of paper towels. Let the tomatoes drain for about 30 minutes.
- Remove the puff pastry from its packaging and let it thaw at room temperature for 30 minutes while the tomatoes drain. Meanwhile, preheat the oven to 400° F and line a baking sheet with parchment paper.
- Unfold the puff pastry onto the parchment-lined baking sheet, and use your fingertips to gently pinch the seams closed. Use a knife to score about a 1/4 inch border all the way around, then copiously prick the crust inside the border with a fork.
- Spread a thin layer of mustard all over the dough, leaving the border bare. Sprinkle the thyme leaves evenly over the mustard. Arrange the tomato slices on top, and season with salt and pepper. Cut small pieces of Brie and scatter them over the top of the tomatoes.
- Bake the tart for 25-30 minutes, or until the crust is puffed and golden and the cheese is melted. Remove from the oven and transfer the tart, on the parchment paper, to a cooling rack to cool for at least 10 minutes. Slice and serve warm or at room temperature.

93. Tropical Mango Salsa With Proscuitto Wrapped Shrimp

Serving: Serves 6 | Prep: | Cook: | Ready in:

Ingredients

- Tropical Mango Salsa
- 2 tablespoons fresh cilantro, rough chop
- 1/2 cup sweet red bell pepper, diced
- 6 tablespoons lime juice, freshly squeezed, divided
- mango 1 large, diced
- 1/2 cup papaya
- 2 jalepenos, seeds removed
- 1/2 cup red onion, diced
- Proscuitto Wrapped Shrimp
- 24 thinly slices proscuitto
- 24 thinly siced ripe melon
- 24 shrimp, cleaned and deveined, shells removed
- 24 tablespoons brie cheese

Direction

- For the salsa, combine all salsa ingredients in a bowl, cover and chill. Use 3 tablespoons of the lime juice, the other 3 marinate the shrimp in, cover and chill.
- For the wrapped shrimp. Lay one piece of prosciutto flat, put a piece of melon in the middle, top with a shrimp, then 1 tablespoon of brie. Wrap the prosciutto around all the filling. Serve with salsa.

94. Turkey, Brie & Peach Panini

Serving: Serves 6 | Prep: | Cook: | Ready in:

Ingredients

- Peach Chutney
- 3 ounces dried peaches, roughly chopped
- 1 garlic clove, minced
- 1/2 small yellow onion, thinly sliced
- 1 cup water
- 1/4 cup apple cider vinegar
- 2 tablespoons light brown sugar
- 1/2 teaspoon kosher salt
- 1/4 teaspoon cayenne
- Panini
- 12 slices crusty bread
- Nonstick cooking spray

- 6 tablespoons country Dijon mustard
- 12 slices roasted turkey breast
- 6 ounces Brie cheese, thinly sliced
- 1-1/2 cups arugula

Direction

- Make the Peach Chutney: In medium saucepan, combine all ingredients. Heat to boiling over medium-high heat. Reduce heat to medium-low; simmer uncovered 25 minutes or until most liquid is absorbed. Let cool. This step can be done up to 1 week in advance. Store chutney in airtight container in refrigerator until ready to use.
- Make the Paninis: Spray 1 side of each bread slice with cooking spray. Spread opposite side of 4 bread slices with mustard. Over mustard, place turkey, brie, Peach Chutney and arugula. Place remaining bread slices, sprayed side up, over arugula.
- Preheat panini press or pan over medium heat. Cook sandwiches until bread is golden brown and cheese melts, about 3 minutes per side, pressing down occasionally with large spatula.

95. Watercress, Pear, And Brie Salad

Serving: Makes 4 small or 2 large | Prep: | Cook: | Ready in:

Ingredients

- 1 shallot, thinly sliced
- 1 tablespoon plus 1 teaspoon extra virgin olive oil
- 1 tablespoon rice wine vinegar
- 3/4 tablespoon fresh lemon juice
- salt and several cranks of freshly ground black pepper
- 1 bunch watercress, washed, stems removed (about 1 1/2-2 cups)
- 2 Seckel pears, sliced crosswise
- 6 Medjool dates, pitted and slivered
- 4 ounces brie, thinly sliced (the thin rind is edible)
- 2 tablespoons toasted pecans, slivered

Direction

- Sauté shallots in 1 teaspoon olive oil for 3-5 minutes, or until softened. Remove from heat and set aside.
- For the dressing, whisk remaining 1 tablespoon olive oil with vinegar, lemon juice, salt, and pepper in a small bowl and set aside.
- To make individual salads, start by placing some watercress in the center of a plate, then add pear slices, the cooked shallots, some brie, and some dates. Top with toasted pecans and drizzle with dressing. Repeat with remaining three dishes.

96. White Cheddar Fig Grilled Cheese

Serving: Makes 2 sandwiches | Prep: | Cook: | Ready in:

Ingredients

- 2 pieces eveything bagel thins
- 1 tablespoon butter
- 2 tablespoons fig preserves
- 4 slices white cheddar cheese
- 6 slices brie (from a brie cheese wheel)
- 1/2 cup arugula

Direction

- Preheat George Foreman grill.
- Separate bagels and add butter to one side. Set aside.
- Slice brie cheese. I lay the wheel down so it is flat and cut 6 pieces. The pieces should be about an inch wide. Trim off the rind.
- If using a skillet, set heat to medium high. Lay one side of bagel thin on grill/skillet. Add one slice of white cheddar cheese, a thin layer of fig preserves (so it is coated, but not

overflowing), three pieces of brie and the second slice of white cheddar. Top with bagel thin top. Repeat with other sandwich.
- Close George Foreman grill and cook for 4-5 minutes. Sandwich is done when cheese is melted. If using a skillet, heat 4-5 minutes on one side and flip. Cook for 4-5 more minutes.
- Lift one bagel thin top and had a small handful of arugula; repeat on other side.
- Serve immediately.

97. Wild Mushroom Onion Galette With Brie

Serving: Serves 8 and a dog (as a starter) | Prep: | Cook: | Ready in:

Ingredients

- 1 large onion - peeled and sliced
- 1 large shallot - peeled and sliced
- 2 tablespoons unsalted butter
- 2 tablespoons olive oil
- 1 1/2 cups mixed wild mushrooms (we used beech, crimini, and oyster) - cleaned and chopped
- 1/2 cup dried porcini mushrooms - chopped
- 1/2 cup dry white wine
- 1 tablespoon minced fresh rosemary
- 1 sheet all butter puff pastry (we used Dufour) - thawed
- 1/2 pound brie - crust removed
- flaked salt (we used maldon)
- salt and pepper
- bulb onions sliced lengthwise - white and some green parts
- drizzle of olive oil
- melted unsalted butter (a tablesoon or so)

Direction

- Put the dried mushrooms and wine in a heat proof something and nuke for a minute to soften. Set them aside. Heat the butter and oil in a medium skillet. When the butter is melted and bubbling hot, add onions, shallots, and a pinch of salt. Cook, stirring often, until they are browned and caramel-ey.
- Using a slotted spoon, remove the onions to a bowl. Add in all of the mushrooms along with the wine to the same pan with the remaining fat. Season with salt and pepper and cook until they are soft.
- Preheat the oven to 400. Lay the puff pastry on a sheet of parchment on a cookie sheet. Arrange the onions and mushrooms on the pastry, leave a 2" border. Sprinkle the rosemary over. Now cut the brie into chunks and arrange on top. Gently fold the edges of the pastry up and over the perimeter. The vegetables will be only partially covered. Arrange the bulb onions lengthwise on top of the exposed vegetables. Drizzle the onions with olive oil. Brush the crust with melted butter, then sprinkle with the entire tart with sea salt. Bake until the crust is puffed and golden brown, about 25 minutes.
- Cool for a few minutes so it can set, but serve warm. Enjoy with friends.

98. Yellow Oyster Mushrooms On A Brie Toast

Serving: Makes 4 toasts | Prep: | Cook: | Ready in:

Ingredients

- 7 ounces mixed oyster mushrooms
- 3 tablespoons butter
- 2 cloves garlic, crushed (or 6 garlic scapes, chopped)
- 1 tablespoon withe wine (optional)
- 4 sprigs fresh thyme
- 4 slices of thick crusted bread, toasted
- 4 ounces good quality Brie cheese (like Delice De Bourgogne)

Direction

- Brush the mushrooms with a dry brush to remove any dirt and tear the large mushrooms into about 1-inch pieces. Heat a large nonstick pan over medium high heat, when nice and hot add the butter, mushrooms and salt. Cook for 2 minutes, stir and add the garlic scapes and the wine (if using). Cook for 1-2 additional minutes until the edges of the mushrooms turn golden brown. Add thyme leaves and set aside.
- Heat the broiler. Cut the Brie cheese into about 1/4-inch (5-6 mm) slices. Top the toasts with the Brie and 1/4 of the mushroom mixture. Arrange the toasts on a baking sheet and place them under the broiler. Bake for 1-2 minutes, or until the Brie has slightly melted and has browned on the edges. Since ovens vary, check toasts often or you might end up with totally melted or burnt toasts.
- Pour yourself a nice glass of chilled Sauvignon Blanc and enjoy!

99. Brie, Pear And Arugula Sandwich

Serving: Serves 2 | Prep: | Cook: | Ready in:

Ingredients

- 1 french baguette
- 1 forelle pear, or any kind you like thinly sliced
- 1/4 pound french brie cheese
- 1 handful arugula leaves, cleaned
- 1/2 lemon, juiced
- 2 tablespoons extra-virgin olive oil
- salt and pepper

Direction

- Cut the baguette in half, set aside half of it for another use. Cut the half into two pieces and filled the baguette w pieces of brie, sliced pears and arugula leaves on top. Make a vinaigrette w lemon, extra-virgin olive oil, salt and pepper, spoon some over the arugula.

100. Pom.brie.crostini

Serving: Makes 4 pieces | Prep: | Cook: | Ready in:

Ingredients

- 2 cloves garlic, chopped large
- 6 tablespoons olive oil
- 1 pinch herbs de provence
- 4 pieces crusty bread or baguette
- 4-6 pieces brie, enough to cover bread
- 1 pomegranate, seeded (enough to cover the brie)

Direction

- In a small saucepan, heat garlic, olive oil and herbs until flavor comes out of garlic.
- Toast bread, brush with oil (leaving the garlic cloves in the pan), until just coated, but not saturated.
- Top with pomegranate and Brie (in either order, I went cheese then pom, but suit yourself) and toast again until cheese is melted.

101. Toasty TBBB

Serving: Serves 5 | Prep: | Cook: | Ready in:

Ingredients

- 1 baguette
- 1 wheel of brie
- 1 bunch basil
- 3-4 tomatoes, sliced
- good quality olive oil

Direction

- Preheat the oven to 450 degrees. Slice the baguette and spread brie over each piece of bread. Then stack a slice of tomato and a basil leaf on top. Drizzle with a little olive oil and arrange on a baking sheet. Bake for about 5 minutes at 450 degrees.

Index

A
Almond 3,5,46
Anise 46
Apple 3,4,11,18,33,40,46,47
Apricot 3,13
Asparagus 3,5
Avocado 3,4,23,42

B
Bacon 3,4,38,47
Baguette 3,15,28
Balsamic vinegar 15,52
Barley 3,29
Basil 3,4,37,39,48,52
Berry 3,4,10,46
Blueberry 3,10
Bran 44
Bread 4,31,39,41,47,49
Brie 1,3,4,5,6,7,8,9,10,11,12,13,14,15,16,17,18,19,20,21,22,23,24,26,27,28,29,30,31,32,33,34,35,36,37,38,39,40,41,42,43,44,45,46,47,48,49,52,53,54,55,56
Brioche 3,16,18
Broth 43
Brown sugar 15
Buckwheat 3,17
Buns 3,24
Burger 3,23,32
Butter 3,5,13,18,24,27,44,46

C
Cake 4,39,46
Camembert 49
Caramel 3,4,6,18,27,28,39
Cardamom 7
Carrot 3,31
Cava 3,19,52
Chard 3,17
Cheddar 3,4,38,54
Cheese 3,4,10,19,27,38,46,51,54
Cherry 3,15,31,52
Chicken 3,4,32,43
Chickpea 3,31
Chipotle 3,15,22
Chutney 3,15,53,54
Cinnamon 7,18,22,46,47
Cloves 7,44,47,48,52
Crackers 9
Cranberry 3,4,20,21,22,41
Cream 3,12,13,22,23,46
Croissant 3,23
Crostini 3,4,14,49
Cumin 31
Currants 22

D
Date 3,4,7,12,14,46
Dijon mustard 6,53,54
Duck 3,23

E
Egg 46
English muffin 32

F
Fennel 3,4,23,45
Fig 3,4,12,13,26,27,54
Flour 10,46,47
French bread 30,38,49

Fruit 3,15,27

Fusilli 3,28

G

Garlic 3,4,24,31,37,41,42,43,44,48,52

Gratin 3,34

H

Ham 3,38

Honey 3,13,17,23,29,32,35,46

J

Jam 3,12,14,27,48

Jus 40,49

K

Kale 3,29,36

L

Leek 3,22,24,34

Lemon 44,48

Ling 4,48

M

Manchego 45,46

Mango 4,53

Marmalade 3,22

Milk 46

Muffins 42

Mushroom 3,4,6,34,36,55

Mustard 3,15,24,31

N

Nut 3,15

O

Oil 4,31,39,48

Olive 14,31,34,48,52

Onion 3,4,6,14,27,31,39,40,43,45,55

Orange 3,27

Oyster 4,55

P

Parmesan 48,49,52

Parsley 44,49

Pasta 3,4,37,48,52

Pastry 3,8,12,18,35,36

Peach 4,48,53,54

Pear 3,4,13,18,23,27,28,32,33,38,45,54,56

Pecan 20

Peel 11,33,34,42,44

Pepper 5,7,22,23,31,48,52

Pesto 3,29

Pie 3,7,33

Pineapple 3,4,33,44

Pistachio 3,8,29,35

Pizza 3,4,14,26,51

Polenta 4,39

Port 4,51

Potato 3,34

Prosciutto 3,14,26,27,38

Pulse 11,18,36,45

Pumpkin 4,39

R

Raspberry 3,13,14

Risotto 3,5,10

Rosemary 3,9,26

S

Salad 3,4,29,31,34,54

Salsa 4,33,53

Salt 5,6,10,15,22,24,31,32,42,45,48,52

Savory 4,45,46,49

Sherry 47

Shin 45

Soup 3,4,22,24,36,43

Steak 4,48

Stock 10

Sugar 22,46,47

Sumac 3,8

Sweetbread 4,49

Swiss chard 17

T

Tea 7,36

Tomato 3,4,19,28,30,31,37,44,48,52

Turkey 4,41,53

V

Vanilla extract 46

Veal 49

Vinegar 31,47

W

Walnut 4,41,46

Watercress 4,54

White pepper 24

Wine 3,10,31,36

Z

Zest 42

Conclusion

Thank you again for downloading this book!

I hope you enjoyed reading about my book!

If you enjoyed this book, please take the time to share your thoughts and post a review on Amazon. It'd be greatly appreciated!

Write me an honest review about the book – I truly value your opinion and thoughts and I will incorporate them into my next book, which is already underway.

Thank you!

If you have any questions, **feel free to contact at:** author@rosemaryrecipes.com

Debora Molino

rosemaryrecipes.com

Printed in Great Britain
by Amazon